A Narrative Of Service With The Third Wisconsin Infantry

by

Julian Wisner Hinkley

Double 9 BOOKS

A Narrative Of Service With The Third Wisconsin Infantry

by Julian Wisner Hinkley

ISBN: 978-93-71469-79-1

Published by

DOUBLE 9 BOOKS

2/13-B, Ansari Road
Daryaganj, New Delhi – 110002
info@double9books.com
www.double9books.com
Tel. 011-40042856

ABOUT THE AUTHOR

Julian Wisner Hinkley was born in 1838 and is best known for his detailed accounts of military history, particularly his time as a captain in the Third Wisconsin Infantry during the Civil War. He gained recognition for his first-hand narrative in A Narrative of Service with the Third Wisconsin Infantry, a work that provided insight into the life of soldiers during one of the most defining periods of American history. Hinkley's memoir sheds light on the challenges faced by soldiers, from their training to the brutal realities of combat, while capturing the camaraderie and duty that defined the military experience. His writing stands as a valuable historical document, offering readers a personal glimpse into the life of a Civil War soldier. Hinkley passed away in 1916 at the age of 78, leaving behind a legacy of military history through his poignant and compelling account of wartime service. His contribution continues to serve as an important resource for those studying the Civil War and its profound impact on the nation.

CONTENTS

WISCONSIN HISTORY COMMISSION

(Organized under the provisions of Chapter 298, Laws of 1905, as amended by Chapter 378, Laws of 1907, Chapter 445, Laws of 1909, and Chapter 628, Laws of 1911)

FRANCIS E. McGOVERN
Governor of Wisconsin

CHARLES E. ESTABROOK
Representing Department of Wisconsin, Grand Army of the Republic

REUBEN G. THWAITES
Superintendent of the State Historical Society of Wisconsin

CARL RUSSELL FISH
Professor of American History in the University of Wisconsin

MATTHEW S. DUDGEON
Secretary of the Wisconsin Library Commission

Chairman, Commissioner Estabrook
Secretary and Editor, Commissioner Thwaites
Committee on Publications, Commissioners Thwaites and Fish

EDITOR'S PREFACE

The author of this volume was born at Vernon, Connecticut, on March 12, 1838, of a long line of New England ancestry; he was sixth in order of descent from Governor Thomas Hinkley of Plymouth Colony. Coming to Wisconsin in his eleventh year, Julian grew to young manhood on his father's farm at Waupun and in Portage County. In 1858, our author left the farm and started life for himself—teaching school in winter, and working as a carpenter each summer.

On April 19, 1861, Mr. Hinkley enlisted in the Waupun Light Guard for three months. But the services of the organization were not accepted for that short term by the State military authorities, so on May 8 they were proffered and accepted for the war, and the organization became Company E of the Third Wisconsin Infantry. Hinkley was at the organization appointed First-Sergeant; but on February 6, 1862, he was commissioned Second-Lieutenant of his company, became First-Lieutenant on November 1 following, and on May 4, 1863, took command of the Company as Captain. He continued to serve the Third Wisconsin until its final discharge and payment in Madison on August 26, 1865, but during the last few months of this period was the acting Major of the Regiment. Since the war, Major Hinkley has been largely engaged in erecting public buildings, and has a wide acquaintance throughout Northeast Wisconsin.

The Commission is much pleased at this opportunity to publish Major Hinkley's *Narrative*. The book has only in part been written from memory. It has been made up from several excellent sources: (1) A manuscript diary kept from day to day, or week to week, by Mr. Hinkley during the years of his service; (2) several contemporary letters written by him, either to the local press of his section of the State, or to relatives and friends at home; and lastly (3), a manuscript narrative written by the author several years after the war, for the edification of his children. The work of amalgamating these diverse materials has fallen to the lot of the editorial department of the Commission; the result, however, has been passed upon in detail by Major

Hinkley, and in its present continuous form accepted by him as his final narrative. This method of compilation has secured a manuscript possessing a contemporaneous flavor and accuracy, not usual with reminiscences. The Commissioners feel that the book is an interesting and valuable contribution to the literature of the war, being the view-point of a company commander in one of the most active of Wisconsin regiments, throughout the entire period of the struggle.

R. G. T.

Wisconsin Historical Library

September, 1912

SERVICE WITH THE THIRD WISCONSIN INFANTRY

Enlistment and Training

The presidential election of 1860 found me just become of age. I exercised my newly-acquired rights of citizenship, in the then little village of Waupun, Wisconsin, by participating in the hurrahing and torchlight processions that in those days characterized a political campaign. I was a carpenter by trade, but immediately after the election went to teach a country school in the backwoods town of Buena Vista, in Portage County. Daily papers in that sparsely settled community were of course an unknown luxury, and it was only through the weeklies that we heard of the gathering storm in the Nation. From them we learned how State after State in the South were holding conventions, that they were passing ordinances of secession, and that the delegates were gathering at Montgomery, Alabama, to organize the Confederate States of America.

In the North, few people seemed as yet to realize that a great war was impending. The Southern newspapers boastfully asserted that secession might be accomplished in peace, for the Northerners were a nation of shopkeepers and mechanics, who would never fight to prevent it. And these statements, reprinted in the Northern papers, were far from soothing, for there is nothing that so quickly arouses the combativeness of men, and especially of young men, as the intimation that they are cowards. Thus were the younger and more hot-headed men on both sides being stirred to warlike feeling by newspaper writers, until such hostile sentiment was aroused that war was inevitable.

Immediately after the secession of South Carolina, I had expressed my intention, in conversation with my friends, that should war follow, I would have a hand in it. This determination grew as events drifted on from bad to worse. I cannot say that I was very strongly animated by a love for the Union in the abstract, or that I considered the abolition of slavery worth fighting for; but I felt that the dismemberment of the Union by armed force, submitted to without a struggle, would be a disgrace to the whole North.

The events of the following winter and spring are a part of the history of the Nation. Abraham Lincoln was inaugurated on March 4, 1861. On April 12, Fort Sumter was fired upon, and surrendered on the 14th. On April 15 Lincoln issued his call for troops, and the war had burst upon the Nation in all its fury.

Waupun for a number of years maintained an independent military company, called the Waupun Light Guard. This organization had in its possession forty stand of arms belonging to the State, and uniforms for about twenty of its members. On the morning of April 19, I had gone down to the main street of the village to buy a paper. While discussing with Captain Clark of the military company, the events of the day, an agent of the State, who had just arrived on the morning train, approached us. He read to the Captain a notice that his company must at once be filled up to the regulation standard and reported for active duty, or surrender its arms, to be used by other companies going into service.

I had not heretofore belonged to this company, but at once told the Captain that I would enlist, and aid him to fill his command to the required standard. A meeting was called for that night, and with the assistance of the patriotic people of the village and surrounding country, the company was filled up by nine o'clock of the next morning. A telegram was immediately sent to Madison, tendering service for the ninety-day call. We had acted promptly and swiftly, yet not quite swiftly enough. Twenty-three other companies had filed notice before us, and the quota of Wisconsin was full.

Enthusiasm among the men ran high, however, and when on May 8 it was learned that no more ninety-day men could be accepted, it was determined by vote to tender service for the entire war, however long that might be. Those whose business was such that they could not leave home for longer than ninety days retired, but their places were quickly taken by others who were anxious to go. We were now accepted, and assigned to the Third Wisconsin Volunteers and ordered to rendevouz at Fond du Lac as soon as camp equipage could be furnished.

The former officers of the company were retained, with the consent of the newly-enlisted men, and additional non-commissioned officers were elected. Among the latter I was chosen First Sergeant, which position I held until promoted to a Second-Lieutenancy.

We boarded at the best hotels in the village, until ordered into camp. We were drilled several hours each day, and prepared for the work in store for us by the study of tactics and army regulations. At length, after what seemed to us in our impatience an interminable delay, we went into camp at Fond du Lac on June 15, and for the first time lived in tents. We now had daily company and battalion drill, together with officers' school in tactics and sword exercise. Colonel Thomas H. Ruger, our commander, was a West Point graduate, and under his efficient direction we became, before we had been very long in the service, as thoroughly drilled and disciplined as any regiment of regulars. Indeed we all felt sure, while we were still at Fond du Lac, that we were already veterans.

On June 28 appeared Captain McIntyre of the regular army to inspect us and muster us into the service of the United States. And here occurred a difficulty which illustrates how confidently the people of the North expected that the war would be of only short duration. Many of the best men in the company, who had been entirely willing to enlist "for the war," objected to being mustered in for a three-years' term of service as required by the instructions of the Federal Government. It was only after considerable persuasion that they were all finally induced to do so. Probably not one of them had the slightest idea that he would serve for three years, and then enlist again for another three years, before the great struggle would be ended.

On the day after mustering in, uniforms were issued to us, consisting of light-grey trousers, mixed-grey blouse, and light-coloured hat. At first, they looked bright and fine, but they were of such poor quality, especially the trousers, that within ten days it was necessary to furnish the entire regiment with common blue workingmen's overalls, in order that we might with decency be seen upon the streets. Some money-loving patriot contractor had gathered in his reward from the State of Wisconsin by providing us with shoddy clothes; and in the end it came out of the pay of the Regiment.

Departure for the Front

The preparations for departure were soon completed, and on July 12, 1861, we shouldered our knapsacks, strapped on our haversacks, containing several days' rations, and boarded the railroad cars for the seat of war in Virginia. The train of twenty-four coaches pulled out of the station amid the cheers and farewells of our many friends, who had gathered to see us off. All were in the best of spirits. It seemed to us as though we were setting out on a grand pleasure excursion. No thought of death or disaster appeared to cross the mind of anyone. And yet how many were saying farewell, never to return!

Our route took us through Chicago, Toledo, Cleveland, and Erie. Everywhere we were feasted and toasted by the enthusiastic people along the line. At Buffalo the entire population seemed to have turned out to welcome the wild woodsmen of the Northwest. The local military companies of that city escorted us through the principal streets; speeches were made by the mayor and prominent citizens. We were very soon convinced that we were, indeed, heroes in embryo. At Williamsport, Pennsylvania, we were given a reception surpassing anything that had gone before; even now, more than fifty years after, its pleasant recollections still linger in my mind. Tables were set along the sidewalk in the shade of magnificent trees, and these tables were literally loaded with all the good things that could tempt an epicure. There were, besides, fair ladies without number to welcome us, and wait upon our needs.

On July 16 we reached Hagerstown, Maryland, where we went into camp, and where on the next day we were equipped with a complete outfit of muskets, ammunition, and camp utensils. The degree of preparation of the Federal Government for war at this time, may be judged from the fact that the muskets issued to us were old-time smooth-bore Springfields, that had been rifled for a minie-ball; they were so light, that their barrels would spring after the rapid firing of a dozen shots.

Service in Maryland

On the morning of July 17 we broke camp and started for Harpers Ferry, thirty miles distant. Now for the first time I began to realize what it was to be a soldier. I carried a knapsack laden with the various things that kind friends at home had thought necessary for a soldier's comfort, a haversack containing two days' rations, a musket with accoutrements, and forty rounds of ammunition, altogether weighing not less than fifty pounds. The weather was extremely hot and the roads very muddy, so that by the time we had gone fifteen miles I was entirely ready to go into camp.

Our camp was pitched on the side of a hill. Our mess, in order to find as level a sleeping place as possible, pitched the tent in a low place, and in our ignorance of camp life we neglected to dig a ditch around it. A sudden shower came up soon after we had gone to sleep, and in a short time we found ourselves lying in a pool of water. And as if this were not misfortune enough, our tent pins, loosened by the soaking of the ground, suddenly pulled out, and down came our canvas shelter. Subsequent experience enabled me to sleep in wet blankets, or in no blankets at all, just as well as in the best bed; but at this time it was impossible. So gathering a rubber blanket around my shoulders, I found a large stone, and remained upon it for the rest of the night. In the morning we continued the march toward Harpers Ferry. Our camp for the next night was pitched on a bit of comparatively level ground on the east side of Maryland Heights, overlooking the little village of Sandy Hook, and about a mile distant from Harpers Ferry. A more thoroughly used-up lot of men than ours that night, it would be hard to find.

My first military duty was to guard the ford at Harpers Ferry and the bridges across the canal. The region was historic ground, and I took this opportunity to visit the old arsenal, then in ruins, and the old engine-house where John Brown had battled so bravely for his life. I made it a point also to visit Jefferson's Rock, the view from which Jefferson, in his *Notes on Virginia*, says is worth a voyage across the Atlantic to see.

On September 15, while encamped in the vicinity of Darnestown, we were ordered, late in the day, to break camp and take the road toward the west. Our destination was not disclosed to us, and there was a great deal of speculation among the men as to the object of this secret and hurried march. The next day we found out from citizens along the road that we were on the way to Frederick City, the capital of Maryland. We arrived there late on the afternoon of the 16th, and received an enthusiastic welcome from the citizens of that loyal town. Early the next morning, guards were stationed on all roads leading out of town, and detachments of men, accompanied by detectives, proceeded to arrest the members of the Maryland Legislature, who had assembled there for the purpose of passing an ordinance of secession. It was thus that Maryland was saved to the Union by the promptness of General McClellan. Her secessionist legislators found themselves, shortly after, assembled at Fort McHenry, with leisure to meditate upon their schemes.

The Regiment remained in camp at Frederick City until late in October. The usual monotony of camp life, with its drills, dress parades, and guard mountings, was broken only by the arrival of the paymaster with crisp new greenbacks of the first issue, and by the appearance of new blue uniforms in exchange for our tattered array. To the old grey we bade adieu without a sigh of regret, and proudly donned the blue of United States soldiers.

One interesting incident occurred during our stay here, which gave us a subject for discussion for several days. News had been brought to us of a large quantity of wheat, stored in a mill in Harpers Ferry, which was about to be ground into flour for the use of the Confederate army. An expedition to capture it was soon organized under command of Colonel John W. Geary of the Twenty-Eighth Pennsylvania. It was composed of a detachment of two hundred men from our regiment under command of Captain Bertram, with similar detachments from the Twelfth Massachusetts and Twenty-Eighth Pennsylvania, besides a section of artillery. The expedition was successful; the wheat was safely removed to the north side of the river, and the command was ready to return, when a large force of the enemy appeared, seemingly disposed for a fight. Our men were quite willing to accommodate them, and moved up the hill toward Bolivar Heights, where the enemy was already strongly posted with artillery. Skirmishing immediately commenced. But this soon proved too slow for our impatient men; they charged the Confederate position, and soon had the satisfaction of seeing the last of the Southerners disappear in the direction of Charlestown, leaving their artillery in our hands.

In this engagement the heaviest fighting fell to the detachment of the Third Wisconsin; the piece of artillery was brought off by them as a trophy. This command also sustained all of the loss, having had six men killed and four wounded. The dead were brought back and buried with military honors in the cemetery at Frederick City. The fight had in a large measure been unnecessary, for the entire object of the expedition had been accomplished before the enemy appeared in force; yet the moral effect on the men was good, since it increased their self-confidence.

On November 1 we rejoined the Division of General Banks, near Darnestown, where we remained until the beginning of the next month. The whole Division then moved to the vicinity of Frederick City, our Regiment being detailed in the city as provost guard. We built our barracks in the old barrack yard, and settled down for the winter to the regular routine of guard duty. Two companies were detailed each day—one for the guard-house, the other to patrol the city and preserve order. The snow, rain, and mud kept the ground in such condition that drilling was impossible; thus we had little to do but kill time with chess, checkers, cards, and dominoes. The winter wore slowly away in this uneventful manner. In January news was received of the victory of General Thomas at Somerset, Kentucky; also the capture of Roanoke Island, by General Burnside, and immediately after this, in February, the great victories of General Grant at Forts Henry and Donelson. The enthusiasm of the command over these successes knew no bounds, and our impatience to be on the move could scarcely be restrained.

On the trail of Stonewall Jackson

At length the long-wished-for came. On the morning of February 25, 1862, we bade adieu to the barracks that had sheltered us so long, and boarding the cars moved to Sandy Hook, where we went into camp on the ground that we had left six months before. During the night there arrived a train of cars with a pontoon bridge, in charge of a detachment of United States engineers; and General McClellan came from Washington by special train, personally to supervise the movement. Our Regiment being largely composed of lumbermen and raftsmen from northern Wisconsin, who were accustomed to running rafts on the rivers of our State, readily made up a detail of a hundred experienced fellows to assist the engineers in laying the bridge. By noon it was constructed, 1300 feet long, in a swift current and our Regiment, the advance of the army, was on its way into Dixie.

We moved rapidly on to Bolivar Heights without seeing anything of the enemy, and halted there for the night, happy in the thought that at last we were doing something. On February 28 a strong reconnoitering party of infantry, artillery, and cavalry, moved forward, and without opposition occupied Charlestown. It was a village of national reputation at that time, for there John Brown was tried and hung. It was one of the hottest secessionist spots in the State, any Union sentiment that might have existed, being carefully concealed. We remained there for several days quartered in the various churches and public buildings, while I improved the opportunity to visit the many points of interest. On March 2 came my commission as Second Lieutenant of Company D.

On March 11 we once more moved forward in the direction of Winchester, the advance guard skirmishing with the enemy occasionally, but meeting no serious resistance. The next morning we turned out at four o'clock, and advancing through fields and woods for about an hour, came at length in sight of the entrenchments of Winchester, about a mile to the front. Our right and left companies were thrown forward as skirmishers, in preparation for a fight, but met with no resistance, and were soon clambering over the parapet of the deserted fort. They pushed on into the town, the remainder of the Regiment following closely after, and received from the mayor the formal surrender of the municipality. It was the first surrender of this interesting city, which is said to have been captured and recaptured more than thirty times during the war. We found here an apparently strong Union sentiment. As our Regiment marched in with colors flying and band playing, the citizens were rejoicing everywhere over their deliverance from the Confederates. Innumerable handkerchiefs were waving to welcome us, and in some instances the stars and stripes were displayed. We learned from citizens that General Stonewall Jackson had with 6,000 men, retreated the night before toward Strasburgh, taking with him quite a number of the Union citizens of the town.

We now went into camp a short distance south of Winchester, where we remained until March 22. Continually we were hearing of the glorious successes of the Western Army, and becoming more and more anxious that our Army of the Potomac should be given an opportunity to rival its achievements. A number of changes in the organization of the Division were made while we were here in camp. The only one of importance to us was the transfer of the Second Massachusetts to our Brigade in place of the Ninth New York, giving us Colonel Gordon of the Second Massachusetts as brigade commander in place of General Hamilton, our old leader. This circumstance was little liked at the time; but it was the beginning of our friendship with the Second Massachusetts, that remained very close throughout the war.

On March 22 our Division left Winchester to proceed, as we believed, to Manassas Junction. At the end of a two days' march we were camping for the night about three miles east of Snicker's Gap, in the Blue Ridge. Rumors here began to circulate, that there had in our absence been considerable fighting at Winchester. It was reported that the Confederates had been defeated, but that General Shields had been wounded in the battle. We were not, therefore, surprised, the next morning, to be ordered to march back over the identical road upon which we had come. We reached Winchester the same night after a hard march of twenty-five miles, and learned from its citizens that there certainly had been a fight. We were informed that General Jackson had learned of our departure from Winchester, but had not heard that Shields was still encamped north of the city. Jackson had made a hasty move to recapture Winchester, but had been confronted by Shields near Kernstown. Here the Confederates had been completely routed and driven beyond Strasburgh, with heavy loss in killed and prisoners.

On the morning after our arrival at Winchester, I went out to take a view of the battle-field, and was able to gain some idea of what the future held in store for us. The wounded had already been cared for, and some of the dead had been buried; but sixteen of our dead remained on the field, and something over three hundred of the enemy's. In one part of the battle-ground, covered with small timber and underbrush, where the enemy had for a time made a stubborn resistance, scarcely a bush or a tree but showed the marks of bullets at a height of from three to six feet from the ground. In my inexperience, I then wondered how any man could have lived in that thicket; and in truth, not many did live there long, for the ground was strewn with the dead.

Returning to camp at noon, I found that we were again under orders to march. We started out near sundown, moving that night to Strasburgh, and found the bridge over Cedar Creek, two miles this side of Strasburgh, destroyed. It had been burned by Jackson at the time of his first retreat from Winchester. This precaution had in the recent fight proved to be his undoing, for in his hasty flight before Shield's Division, his army, which up to that place had preserved good order, was completely disorganized and suffered a loss of two hundred prisoners.

We remained at Strasburgh for several days. During that time I was detailed on a general court martial to try some soldiers who had been arrested for depredations on private property. Their offence, as I was informed, consisted in stealing chickens and honey, against which stringent orders were at that time in force. The court convened in all dignity, and sent word to the General that it was ready to try the culprits. In a few minutes Adjutant Wilkins appeared, presented the compliments of the General and informed us that the prisoners had escaped. We were requested to adjourn until they had been recaptured. As that court was never reconvened, it may be taken for granted that the prisoners were never recaptured.

On the first day of April we again moved forward, driving the enemy in such haste that they left their dinners cooking on the fires. Several times during the day, they opened on us with artillery, but a few shots from our battery would quickly send them on again. On the 17th we made another attempt to get at Jackson's army, by moving one Division up the Shenandoah River on the west side, and the other into New Market from the southwest. Our Regiment was with the latter Division. After fording a river up to our armpits, and finding it as cold as melting snow from the mountains could make it, we found that the enemy had again shown his heels and once more was away to the south.

During the next month we followed the retreating army of General Jackson to Harrisonburg, and then came back to Strasburgh. Here we made some little show of fortifying; but in the main, we were as easy and unconcerned as though the war was over. And in fact, the good news received from all quarters, and the orders from the War Department to stop all recruiting, led us to believe that the contest was nearly ended. In camp, bets were freely offered, with no takers, that the Regiment would be back in Wisconsin by September. I remember writing to a friend, about this time, that my part of the work of suppressing the Rebellion seemed to be about done. How sadly were we mistaken!

The Tables Turned

We had a rude awakening from our dream of peace. While we had been idling in fancied security, General Jackson had gathered a large force with which to overwhelm us. Our first intimation of trouble came on the night of May 23, when we were hastily called to defend our railroad bridge toward

Front Royal against the attack of the enemy. The next day we were in full retreat toward Winchester.

When about half way to Winchester, the enemy, who had crossed from Front Royal, attacked our train in the front. The Fifth Connecticut and Twenty-Eighth New York were hurried forward, with the rest of the command following, and the road was soon cleared. But this had hardly been accomplished, when the enemy attacked in the rear, and cut off about fifty wagons. At this new danger a halt was called, and with two regiments and a battery, General Banks hastened to the rear. The lost wagons were recovered, but the animals having all been driven off or killed, it was necessary to burn the vehicles. Among the wagons destroyed was one containing all the rations and cooking utensils of my Company. We succeeded at night in securing a few crackers from some of the more fortunate companies, but most of my men went supperless to bed. Moreover, there were prospects for a lively fight in the morning.

I was awakened early by the picket-firing, which commenced at daybreak, and found myself thoroughly chilled from sleeping on the bare ground, without blankets or shelter. However, both hunger and cold were soon forgotten in the more pressing demands upon our attention. The position chosen by General Banks for the night's bivouac was probably the worst that could have been found between Strasburgh and the Potomac River. With seven regiments of infantry we occupied a small field lying between the outskirts of the city and the hills on the south. The enemy were in possession of the hills, where they had erected considerable fortifications. Colonel Gordon's Brigade was on the right of the road; that of Colonel Donnelly was on the left—all facing the enemy.

Our skirmishers were promptly advanced, and commenced firing on the enemy in their entrenchments. Supported by a battery in our rear, which fired over our heads into their position, we were maintaining a lively fire, when suddenly it was discovered that the enemy was passing around upon our right, with the evident intention of getting in our rear. The Twenty-Seventh Indiana and Twenty-Ninth Pennsylvania were hurriedly moved to the right, but had hardly reached their position when they were furiously assailed both in front and flank by the advancing Confederates. The Twenty-Ninth Pennsylvania received the first brunt of the attack, and soon was in full retreat. The Twenty-Seventh Indiana came in for the next attack, and they also fell back about a quarter of a mile to some stone walls on the outskirts of the city. Our Regiment and the Second Massachusetts, which as yet had scarcely been engaged, were now faced about and marched to the rear, until we reached the fenced lots on the outskirts of the town. Here we were halted, and opened fire on the enemy, who had appeared in large numbers upon our front.

We had soon checked the Confederates immediately before us. I was looking around to see how things were going with the others, when I became aware that Company F and a portion of my Company were entirely alone. It appears that orders had been sent around by General Banks to fall back to the north side of the city; but we, being separated from the rest of the Regiment by an intervening street, had not heard them. There we were, fighting the whole Southern army by ourselves! I hastened to Captain Limbocker to call his attention to our position. He saw the situation at a glance, and left-facing the companies, marched double-quick through the back streets toward the main road of the city. By this time our men had discovered that they were in a close place, and moved rapidly. Just as we reached the main street and turned north, I stopped to speak to the Captain, who was in the rear. As I did so, I saw that the whole street behind us to the south was swarming with Confederate soldiers, not fifty feet away. They were in such confusion, however, that it was impossible for them to fire, and in fact they did not seem to try. From that point until we were clear of the street, it was simply a foot race, in which we were the winners. They evidently soon tired of the race, for before we were clear of the street they had some artillery in position, and shot and shell were flying harmlessly over our heads.

We afterwards learned that Colonel Donnelly's Brigade, which at the beginning of the fight had been posted out of our sight on the left of the road, had also, like our Brigade, been assailed in front and in the flank; and that they also, had soon been forced back in full retreat.

We rejoined our Regiment in the line, without further trouble. From our position we could see the enemy on the hills west of us, endeavoring by rapid marching to reach the road in our rear. We stopped only long enough to gather up our men, who had become scattered in coming through the streets of the city, and then moved on toward Martinsburg. We did no more fighting and no more running. All of General Banks's command was ahead of us except two sections of artillery, and detachments of the First Vermont and First Michigan Cavalry, which protected our rear and kept the enemy at a respectful distance. During the retreat, General Banks did all that lay in the power of any man to bring off his men without loss, giving personal attention to the posting of the rear guard.

I suppose it was about eight o'clock in the morning when our Regiment began its march to Martinsburg, twenty-three miles distant. We arrived there at about five in the afternoon, without having stopped for dinner, and without rest. Indeed, we had no dinner to stop for, and the pursuing enemy were not inclined to let us rest. We expected to stop at Martinsburg, but General Banks did not deem it safe, so after a rest of a half hour we were ordered to proceed to Williamsport, Maryland, twelve miles farther on.

We arrived at the Potomac, opposite Williamsport, about ten o'clock that night, tired, hungry, and in no very good humor over the results of our two days' work. We managed to secure some salt pork and a few crackers for supper, after which we wrapped ourselves in our overcoats, and took such rest as could be obtained, amid the noise of men and teams crossing the ferry, and the calls of stragglers who were coming in and seeking their regiments. At three o'clock in the morning we were aroused, and ordered to the ferry. About an hour later we were across the Potomac on the Maryland side, drawn up in line of battle and waiting for the enemy.

General Banks was untiring in his efforts to bring our train over safely, even riding into the water to save mules that had lost their footing, and were in danger of drowning. He made a speech to the men, telling them that the enemy had advanced no farther than Martinsburg, and that 20,000 men had been sent to cut off their retreat.

The roll call taken at this time showed that eleven men of Company D were missing. Four of these came in the next day, having taken a different route than ours through the mountains. Four others turned up in Libby prison. Most of our men had thrown away their knapsacks, some their haversacks and canteens, and sixteen had lost their guns.

We remained at Williamsport until June 10, receiving new supplies of camp and garrison equipage to replace those that had been lost or destroyed.

We were rejoiced during this time to hear that the Confederates had had the tables turned on them; that they were being severely pressed between Shields's and Frémont's armies; and that all the baggage and prisoners that they had captured from us had been retaken, with a good deal more besides.

On the morning of June 10 we again crossed into Virginia, and marched to Front Royal without interruption. We passed through Winchester on the 12th without stopping, however, for the General seemed to fear that our men would burn the town in return for the treachery of its citizens during our retreat. Both men and women had fired on us from the windows, and had poured down scalding water as we passed through the streets. It was even reported to us that women had entered the hospitals, and shot sick men in their beds; but this last was later contradicted.

We remained at Front Royal until July 6, during which time important changes were made in commanding officers. All the troops in northern and western Virginia were united under General John Pope—the three army corps being commanded by McDowell, Sigel, and Banks. A movement was made to concentrate the three corps in one locality east of the Blue Ridge, in the accomplishment of which we were marched over the mountains at Chester Gap on the hottest day I ever experienced. Eight men of my company were sun-struck that afternoon, resulting fatally in one case, and in permanent disability in the others. We camped at night on the headwaters of the Rappahannock, in a country described as naturally poor, and entirely ruined by cultivation. There was one exception to this, however, in the abundance of fruit. There were cherries and blackberries in plenty for everybody.

While in camp near Little Washington, the unfortunate, bombastic orders of General Pope were published to the army; unfortunate, because they incited a degree of contempt for him which greatly impaired his usefulness. Many of his highflown phrases, such as "shame and disaster lurking in the rear," afforded a fine opportunity for the wits of the army, when, not three weeks later, his headquarters wagon and his personal baggage were captured by the enemy. About the first of August he arrived at the front, and on the next Sunday reviewed General Banks's corps. Pope's fine appearance, soldierly bearing, and evident knowledge of his business did much to inspire respect, and might even have made him popular, if we could only have forgotten that fool address to the army. He inaugurated, also, many real reforms. I don't know whether he was entirely responsible for it; but under his command the cavalry began to be of real service to the army, and the men could no longer ask, "Who ever saw a dead cavalryman?"

At Cedar Mountain

On August 7 we broke camp again and marched to Culpeper Court House. Here we learned that the enemy had been seen in considerable force near Cedar Mountain. We were not surprised, therefore, on the morning after our arrival, to be hastily formed and ordered off toward Cedar Mountain. We arrived at Cedar Run in the early afternoon, and found Crawford's Brigade of our Division already skirmishing with the enemy. Our Brigade immediately formed in line of battle on the right of the road, and threw out its skirmish line. At about four o'clock, my Company and four others were moved forward to reënforce the skirmishers.

We had crossed Cedar Run Creek, and were waiting for further orders in a heavy stand of timber, when Captain Wilkins of General Williams's staff rode up, enquiring for General Banks. Lieutenant-Colonel Crane informed him that we had seen nothing of General Banks since we entered the woods. Captain Wilkins then explained to us that General Augur was meeting with considerable success on the left, and that General Crawford desired our Brigade to join his in a charge upon the right. The movement required the sanction of General Banks, who was, however, nowhere to be found, and time was so pressing that he almost felt justified in giving the order himself, as coming from General Banks. Captain Wilkins then turned and rode off, but had not been gone two minutes, and had not, I am confident, seen General Banks, when he returned, and gave Colonel Ruger orders to assemble the Regiment on the right of Crawford's Brigade and charge the enemy's lines.

Our skirmish line was now called in; we formed in line of battle, and marched through the woods as rapidly as the nature of the ground would permit. We had soon come to its edge, and found before us an open field about a hundred and twenty-five yards across, separated from us by a rail fence. Immediately beyond the field, rose the thickly-timbered slope of the mountain; and there too, stationed directly in our front, was a battery of artillery. Of infantry, there were none to be seen.

We hurried forward, pushed down the fence, and without stopping to reform our line started on a run for that battery. I noticed as we went, that Crawford's Brigade had not yet arrived, and that we were alone in the field. Suddenly, from the side of the slope and from the bushes and rocks on our front, arose the Confederate infantry, and poured into our ranks the most destructive musketry fire that I have ever experienced. Lieutenant-Colonel Crane was killed, and fell from his horse at the first volley. Major Scott was wounded, being carried off by his horse. Captain Hawley, of the company on our right, was wounded, and a third of his men were killed or wounded at the same time. The right began to fall back, some of the men helping off wounded comrades, others loading and firing at the enemy as they slowly retreated to the woods. On the left, all three of my companies were standing up to their work without flinching. My Company, though suffering severely, were fighting like veterans. We did not seem to be gaining any advantage, however, and shortly the order came to fall back to the woods. My Company, and that of Captain O'Brien on the left, were the last to leave the field.

Under the shelter of the woods we reformed our companies. I still had about twenty-five men, Captain O'Brien about as many more, and a number of men from Company F had joined me on the right. We at once returned to the edge of the woods, the Colonel leading back the two left companies, and opened fire on the enemy, who was preparing to cross the open field. We soon were sent to the right, however, in order to make room for the Tenth Maine, and saw no more active fighting for that day. At twilight, when we were threatened upon our right flank, we returned across Cedar Run to the ground from which we had started.

Of the 8,000 men that were engaged in this battle, we lost about 2,000 in killed and wounded.

The loss in our Regiment was 117, mostly from the six companies that started in the charge on the battery. Lieutenant-Colonel Crane was killed, and Captain O'Brien mortally wounded. O'Brien had at the first charge been severely wounded in the thigh. When we retreated to the woods, he had showed me that his shoe was full of blood. He had, however, returned to the fight after binding up his wound with his handkerchief, and had been killed at the edge of the woods. My Company had, out of forty-five men engaged, lost two killed and fourteen wounded. Of these all but two of the wounded had been struck in the field where we first drew the enemy's fire, and in a space of time which I am confident did not exceed three minutes.

As some 30,000 or 40,000 troops were in the vicinity, who had not fired a shot, I supposed that the battle would be renewed in the morning; but it was not. The corps of General Sigel and McDowell were moved to the front, but occupied themselves only with gathering up the wounded. On the 11th the enemy sent in a flag of truce, asking for an armistice to bury the dead. This was readily granted, for we also had still on the battle-field many dead and severely wounded. On the 12th it was found that the Confederates had taken advantage of the truce to retreat during the night. Indeed, they retired in such haste that they left large numbers of their wounded in our hands. General Sigel pursued them to the Rapidan, while our Corps returned to Culpeper for a much-needed rest.

A great deal of criticism has been heaped upon all those who were prominently connected with this battle. Banks has been assailed for fighting the battle at all. It has seemed to many, an inexcusable piece of folly that he should have ordered the attack in such apparent ignorance of the position and strength of the enemy, and so near sundown that even if he had been successful, he could not have reaped any advantage. I have, however, doubted whether he ever made the order; but when once it had been made, he was obliged to put in his whole command or abandon everything that had been gained. Captain Wilkins who brought the order for our charge, later wandered into the Confederate lines while carrying orders, and I never heard of him again.

Pope has been criticized for not seeing that Banks was properly supported; but all the evidence obtainable shows that Pope did not wish or expect to fight a battle at that time. McDowell has been criticized with particular bitterness for not going to the aid of Banks, and charges of treachery were freely made against him. It was quite generally believed, even in his own command, that McDowell had no heart in the cause; and this belief—which later gained public expression in the dying statement of Colonel Brodhead of the First Michigan Cavalry, that he "died a victim to the incompetency of Pope and the treachery of McDowell"—caused his retirement as a corps commander.

The Army retreats Northward

We remained at Culpeper until August 18, when we were aroused at midnight and started on the road to the Rappahannock. We crossed over on the next day and went into camp about half a mile from the river. During all that day and night the army of General Pope was streaming across the Rappahannock to the north side, only a portion of his cavalry still remaining to the south. There was a great deal of speculation among the men as to the reason for this unexpected retrograde movement. It was rumored that General McClellan had been compelled to withdraw his army from the Peninsula, and that General Lee, released from the defence of Richmond, was marching our way. For once, rumor was correct. It was not many days before the whole of Lee's army was hunting to find an unguarded point at which to cross the river.

About noon on the day after our crossing, I was watching the movements of some of our cavalry who still remained on the other side of the river. I was standing on the top of one of the highest knolls in the vicinity, from which I had a splendid view of the country for a long distance southward. For nearly two miles the land was clear of timber or fences or any obstacle which could impede the movements of cavalry. Observing that our cavalry seemed to be coming back at rather a livelier pace than usual, I noticed what appeared to be either a large regiment or a small brigade of Confederate cavalry emerge from the woods to the south of the plain. They formed their lines and moved to the attack.

Our men, also, were soon in motion. As they approached each other the two bodies increased their pace, until both seemed to be moving at full speed. They met with a jar, and for some moments it was impossible to distinguish friend from foe. There could only be distinctly seen the flashing of sabres in the sunlight as blows were struck and parried, and the puffs of smoke from revolvers and carbines. For ten minutes or more the stirring fight went on without any apparent advantage to either side. But now another regiment of our cavalry, which had been out of sight up the river at the beginning of the fight, came down upon the Confederates at a hard gallop. It was but a minute before the latter were retreating back to the timber, perhaps hurried a little by a few shells from one of our shore batteries. A little later, I learned that our cavalry had taken about sixty prisoners.

On the night of August 22 the enemy were expected to make an attempt to cross the Rappahannock at Beverly Ford, where I was stationed on picket duty. During the night, however, the river rose almost ten feet as the result of heavy rains in the mountains. By morning, it was so raging a torrent that crossing was impossible. As soon as it was light, the enemy opened fire on us with fourteen pieces of artillery. I had already withdrawn my men from the river bank and stationed them where they could pour a heavy fire upon the Confederates, should they attempt to lay a bridge. I was therefore in a good position to watch at leisure the artillery duel which ensued. For two hours the shot flew back and forth across the stream, without, however, great damage to our side. At the end of that time the Confederates apparently had had enough and withdrew from their position.

The succeeding days were passed in hard marching, with hot weather, no tents or blankets, short rations, and a poor country to forage in. The enemy occasionally made demonstration as though to cross at the fords of the Rappahannock, but all the while moving up toward the mountains. On the evening of August 27, while we were in camp near Warrenton Junction, rumors began to circulate that they had appeared in large force at Manassas Junction, and were threatening to cut off our retreat to Washington. The next morning we were called out at three o'clock, and soon after were on the road to the Junction. The corps of Generals Heintzelman and Fitz-John Porter, which had been marching toward Warrenton, had also been turned back and were directly in our advance. We marched rapidly to Kettle River, a small stream about five miles from the Junction, where we were detailed to guard a train of ninety cars loaded with ammunition and provisions for our army. Here we learned that the enemy had on the previous day captured and destroyed at the Junction over a hundred and fifty cars loaded with supplies, but had in the morning encountered Hooker's advance division near Kettle Run, and had been driven with considerable loss beyond the

Junction. We found on our arrival at Kettle Run, tangible evidence of the morning's fight, for a good many of the dead were still lying around.

Cannonading commenced early on the morning after our arrival, in the direction of Manassas, and continued all day. It was evident that a severe battle was in progress. Reports of our successes were continually coming in; we appeared to be driving the enemy at all points. It was said that the Confederates were surrounded on three sides, and hopes were strong that they would be captured before the main body of their army came up. The next morning, the battle was still in progress although it seemed to be farther away than it had been before. The most encouraging reports continued to reach us, and at night General Pope was credited with having said that our troops had won a complete victory.

While the battle was in progress, we had been occupied in rebuilding the bridge across Kettle Run, which the enemy had destroyed on the first day of their raid. We had it completed, and our train of cars moved across to Bristoe Station by the morning of the second day of the battle. We bivouacked that night north of Broad Run, happy in the thought that our troops had indeed vanquished the foe.

The next morning we were ordered to return to Bristoe. As we approached the station, dense clouds of smoke were rolling upwards from the place where we had left our cars. This gave us notice that the reports of victory had been false. The fact was, that the left wing of Pope's army had been driven back the night before, and it had been necessary to burn the cars in order to prevent their falling into the hands of the enemy. It had been possible to save only the supplies with which they were loaded. Our Corps, moreover, having received no notice of the reverse, was now in grave danger of being cut off from the remainder of the army. We managed, however, by rapid marching over a circuitous route to reach the north side of Bull Run in safety.

The next day we marched to a short distance beyond Centerville. Here we were halted, and stood in the road on our arms during a driving rain, while the battle of Chantilly was being fought only a short distance to the north. We remained standing in the road—or at least were supposed to be standing—all that night, the rain pouring down in torrents most of the time. After darkness had set in, however, the men quietly began to disappear into the neighboring woods, and soon I alone of all my Company was actually standing in the road. I was not greatly troubled over the breach of orders, for I knew that at the first intimation of danger every man would be in his place. I too found for myself as dry a place as possible, and wrapping my rubber coat about me, tried to secure a snatch of much-needed sleep. But

I soon awoke so thoroughly wet and cold that further slumber was out of the question. I thereupon sought a fire that some soldiers had built, and endeavored to extract a bit of comfort from its friendly heat. Just as I was beginning to feel its warmth, a number of staff officers came along and ordered the blaze extinguished, for, said they, it was against the orders of General Banks. I stepped back into the darkness so as not to be recognized, concluding that if General Banks wanted that fire put out, he would get no help from me. The men standing near, however, kicked the burning brands apart as though to put it out, and the officers passed on. But they were not fifty feet away before the fire had been rekindled and was again dispensing cheer. This scene was repeated at frequent intervals until daylight, the fire continuing to burn in spite of all orders.

That morning we took the road about nine, and marched until midnight. On the morning after, we found that we were within the fortifications of Alexandria. Two days later we crossed the Potomac at Georgetown, and went into camp at Tennalleytown, D. C. Our wagons and camp equipage had preceded us. A mail also was awaiting us, the first that we had received since leaving Culpeper Court House.

We now had leisure to reflect upon our situation. It was indeed humiliating. Here we were, after six months of campaigning, back again at the point where we had started. The Grand Army of the Potomac forced to seek the shelter of the fortifications of Washington! The actual fighting had usually been in our favor. Why was it, then, that we had been forced back? We believed that the answer lay entirely in the fact that we had been outgeneralled. We felt that Pope and McDowell were the Jonahs who should go overboard. And overboard they went, not to be heard of again during the war. The reappointment of McClellan to command was everywhere received with pleasure. So far as my acquaintance went, the feeling was unanimous in his favor.

For several days we remained in camp enjoying the luxury of tents and beds after our strenuous experiences on the march. New regiments were in the meantime assigned to the old brigades. Ours received the Thirteenth New Jersey and the One Hundred Seventh New York, with a new corps commander in the person of General Mansfield.

Moving Toward the Enemy

On September 5 it was definitely rumored in camp that the enemy had crossed into Maryland by way of Edward's Ferry. All of the Army of the Potomac were soon after moving up the river toward Darnestown, where a defensive position was taken and the enemy's movements awaited. There were no further developments until the 10th, when an order came from General McClellan to store in Washington all of the officers' baggage and the company tents and property, and turn over the teams to be used in hauling provisions and ammunition. This looked more like business than anything we had yet seen.

The next morning we began to move in earnest, passing through Darnestown, and on toward Frederick City. On the 12th we made a long march to Ijamsville, where we heard from one party of citizens that the enemy were evacuating Frederick City, and from another that they were preparing to fight us at the crossing of the Monocacy River. In the morning, we were early on the road, marching rapidly to the ford of the Monocacy, and crossing without trouble. As we approached Frederick, we could hear the firing of the advance of Burnside's Corps, as they were driving the rear guard of the retreating enemy from the passes of the Catoctin Mountains, about five miles west of the city. Over 800 prisoners were sent back that day, mostly stragglers and deserters, who had soldiered as long as they wished.

That night we camped near Frederick City, a large portion of our Regiment taking advantage of the opportunity to visit old friends and acquaintances in that place. We had been there so long during the past year that it seemed to us almost like home. The Confederates had been in possession for nearly a week, and many stories were told of the good people who had displayed their loyalty under adverse circumstances. The real heroine of the town was old Barbara Fritchie, who had kept a Union flag waving from her window during all the time of the Confederate occupation. Her name has been immortalized by Whittier. I know that in recent years it has been said that no such person ever lived, and that the flag was not displayed. But I heard the story told within twenty-four hours after the Confederate army had left Frederick, from persons who knew the circumstances, and I am going to believe it until there is more positive proof than I have yet seen, that it is not true.

Battle of South Mountain

We were ready to march by four o'clock on the morning of the 14th. But we might as well have stayed in camp until seven. The road west from Frederick was a fine, broad turnpike, wide enough for two or three wagons abreast, but it was now completely choked with the ammunition and provision wagons of the troops in advance. Even after we did finally get started, and were clear of the town, we had to march through the fields and woods on either side of the road.

When we reached the top of the Catoctin Mountains, we could hear the sound of artillery and musketry fire on the next mountain ridge beyond. Occasionally we could even catch a glimpse of the lines of our troops as they moved up the slopes to assault the position of the enemy. We were now rapidly marched down the mountain and turned off by a circuitous route to the right, in order to strike the enemy on the left flank. Before we could reach their position, however, it had already been carried by assault, and the enemy had taken advantage of the darkness to make good their retreat. Such was the battle of South Mountain.

We now countermarched to the turnpike near Middletown, where we went into camp at one o'clock in the morning. We had been on the road for twenty-two consecutive hours, most of the time climbing over rocks and through brush on the mountain side. Again we were on the march, at eight o'clock the next morning, crossing South Mountain as we had crossed the Catoctin Mountains, with the wagon train occupying the road and the troops in the woods along the side. We passed through Boonsborough in the afternoon, and by night had reached nearly to Keedysville.

The road was strewn with the muskets and other accoutrements of the enemy fleeing from South Mountain, together with a great deal of plunder that they had gathered in Maryland. There was every indication that they had retreated in a state of demoralization. The houses in Boonsborough and the vicinity were filled with their wounded, and we were constantly meeting squads of from twenty to one hundred prisoners who were being sent back from the front. Occasional artillery firing in the front seemed to indicate that we were being waited for not far ahead.

Battle of Antietam

On the morning of the 16th we moved forward to a position behind a range of low hills near Antietam Creek, and there we remained until night, undisturbed save by occasional shots from the enemy's batteries, posted in the hills on the opposite side of the creek. The remainder of our army kept coming up all day, taking position as they arrived, until at night it was understood that they were all at hand with the exception of Franklin's Corps, which had gone to the relief of Harpers Ferry. At about nine o'clock we were called up and moved across Antietam Creek, close to the enemy's lines, where we lay down to secure such rest as we might in preparation for the next day's fight. General Hooker's Corps lay in position, just in front of us.

It was reported that night that Harpers Ferry had been surrendered by Colonel Miles without a struggle, and when the relieving force of General Franklin was within three miles. It was rumored also that Miles had been shot by the men of his own command when they learned that they had been surrendered.

We were awakened soon after daylight by the sound of heavy cannonading in the front. It had been raining during the night, but now the sky was clear and the sun shining. The men hurried into the ranks, and the Corps formed in close column by companies. We moved a short distance to the right, then sat down to await developments. As battery after battery came into action, the artillery firing continually increased in rapidity, until for a few minutes the roar would be continuous. Then there would be a lull, and the sharp crack of the musketry would be heard, as the skirmishers pushed forward through the timber. Now the scattering musketry fire increased into crashing volleys; as more and more troops became engaged, the volleys developed into one continuous roar, like the roll of distant thunder.

Within a few minutes we became aware by sight, as well as by sound, that a bloody battle was in progress; a constant stream of wounded men was coming back to the field hospital in the rear. Many were but slightly wounded and still clung to their muskets as they hurried back to have their wounds dressed. They would stop on their way, for a moment, hastily to tell how they were "driving the Johnnies" in the front. Others, more seriously hurt, were being helped along by comrades; while others, still more unfortunate, lay silent on stretchers as they were borne back by ambulance men and musicians. Soon, a number of ammunition wagons which had ventured too close to the front, came dashing by us to seek shelter behind a neighboring hill. They were followed shortly after by a dismounted cannon being dragged back for repairs. Now came a temporary lull in the musketry. The thunder of the artillery increased as if in compensation; but rising above all came the cheers of our comrades in the front, announcing that the opening engagement had ended in victory.

The pause in the musketry was of short duration. The enemy, largely reënforced, soon attacked in their turn, making desperate efforts to regain the ground that they had lost. Upon our side, more troops to the right and left came into action, and the battle was soon raging again with redoubled fury. The enemy in our immediate front seemed to have largely increased their artillery, and scattering shot and shell were dropping around us.

At length our First Brigade was sent into action. We soon followed, at double-quick, in close column by companies. Passing rapidly through the woods, we emerged upon the field a little northeast of the old Dunkard church, and our Regiment deployed in line. The manœuvre was executed as though we had been on a parade ground instead of a battle-field. I have seldom seen it better done.

Immediately on our right and about one hundred yards to the front, was posted one of our batteries of twelve-pound brass guns. It had evidently been in action for some time. All of its horses were killed or crippled, and the gunners were just falling back before the advancing Confederate line of battle. To the left of the battery, and stretching off to the woods directly in our front, stood the remnants of a brigade, still stubbornly contesting the advance of the enemy's infantry. Our Regiment moved forward to the battery, the artillerymen at the same time returning to their guns. The Second Massachusetts took position to the right; the Twenty-Seventh Indiana came up on the left.

The Confederate infantry moved steadily across the corn-field, while the decimated brigade in its path fell back, step by step. We were obliged to wait before commencing fire, until they could be moved out of the way. Then we opened fire from one end of the line to the other. The enemy were handicapped by the fact that they were moving diagonally across our front, instead of directly toward us, and our fire was terribly severe, so it was not long before they broke and ran back to the woods. Immediately, however, another line was coming up, this time confronting us squarely. And now commenced the work in earnest.

Our position was in a stubble-field. The ground in front of us sloped gently downward, so that we were fifteen or twenty feet higher than the enemy. About a hundred yards in our front was a rail fence, beyond which lay another open field. The previous day, that field had contained a luxuriant growth of ripening corn; now it was cut by bullets and trampled by men and horses, until scarce a vestige of the crop remained.

For a time, the enemy came on rapidly, without firing a shot. Their right, like our left, was "in the air" and about even with us. They were as gallant fellows as ever moved to an assault. One could but admire the steady courage with which they approached us; great gaps being made in their lines at every discharge of our grape- and canister-laden twelve-pounders, and our bullets also wore them away at every step. A portion of these stern fighters reached the fence; none came farther. They there stopped and opened fire on our lines. From our higher ground we could see the steady stream of their wounded being helped to the rear. Still they held on, returning fire for fire; and we too were suffering terribly. At length the

Confederates had been reduced to a mere handful; it was hopeless to hold on any longer, and they fell back toward the woods. But before they had reached there, another of their brigades was coming up behind them. The newcomers, however, halted and opened fire at nearly double the distance that their predecessors had taken. Soon they also began to waver, then suddenly broke, and joined their comrades in the flight to the woods.

As they all disappeared toward the timber, General Hooker rode up and ordered us to fix bayonets and pursue. With a whoop and hurrah our Regiment and the Twenty-Seventh Indiana started down through the corn-field, General Hooker himself leading like a captain. It was such traits as this that made him popular, even with those who did not think him fit for high command. We had passed fairly into the corn-field, which was literally strewn with the dead bodies of Confederates, when a staff officer rode up, and ordered us to get out of the way, for General Sumner wished to put in a division at that point. This was all that prevented us from assaulting a position with about a hundred and fifty men, which a few minutes later Sedgwick's Division, with five or six thousand, failed to carry.

We moved back out of the corn-field to our old position, and immediately after Sedgwick's Division came in from the northeast. As they moved forward in perfect line to the attack, they presented a splendid sight, even to old soldiers, and we had little doubt that they would sweep everything before them. They marched in three parallel lines, one behind the other, and about seventy-five yards apart. The brigade and field officers, aware of the peculiar danger of being on horseback in such a place, all marched with their men on foot. The only mounted officer in the entire division was old General Sumner himself, who rode a little in the rear of his first line. He was then nearly seventy years of age, perfectly grey but still proudly erect. As he stretched his tall form to its full height on his horse, in order to see what might be in front of his men, he was the most conspicuous object on the field, and undoubtedly was the target for every Confederate sharpshooter in sight.

No resistance of consequence was met until the advance brigade was out of sight in the woods, and the Second Brigade was just at the edge. Then a heavy musketry fire showed that the enemy had reformed their lines and were making a stubborn fight. Their artillery also now opened fire, and shells and round shot began to fall in our neighborhood. It soon became evident to us, who were spectators of the fight, that General Sumner's formation had been a serious mistake. His second and third brigades were exposed to a heavy fire from the enemy, yet they could not reply on account of the line in front of them. They soon broke up in confusion, therefore, and fell back out of range. The leading brigade held on for over half an hour, to the position that it had gained in the woods, when it also fell back, with but a small portion of the magnificent line which a short time before had so gallantly gone forward to the attack.

The remnant of our Regiment, together with portions of several other like commands, were now stationed at the edge of the woods behind a battery of artillery. There was little more active fighting, however, in that part of the field during the remainder of the day. At one time the enemy made an attempt to recover the lost ground in the corn-field, but the batteries easily drove them back to the woods. Soon after twelve o'clock we were relieved by fresh troops and moved a short distance to the rear. With the friendly aid of a rail fence we now built a fire, and prepared our dinner of hardtack and coffee, and remained quiet for the rest of the day. To the left the firing continued until late in the afternoon.

Many of our gallant boys laid down their lives that bloody day on the battle-field of Antietam. In the morning, our Regiment had taken into the fight twelve officers and not quite 300 enlisted men. The number was thus small because our wounded from Cedar Mountain had not yet rejoined us, and hard marching had sent others to the hospital. Of the twelve officers, we lost one killed and seven severely wounded. The Colonel had been hit in the head by a bullet, which had cut just deep enough to draw blood; while I had received a severe bruise from a spent ball. Of our 300 privates, we lost 194 in killed and wounded. The Twenty-Seventh Indiana on our left, had lost about half of its men; the Second Massachusetts on the right, had suffered in about the same proportion.

In my Company, of the thirty men whom I took into the field, two had been killed, two mortally wounded, and sixteen so severely hurt, that they were ordered to the hospital. Of all that Company, only one had escaped without the mark of a bullet upon his person or his clothes. Every one of our color-guard, composed of a corporal from each company, had been shot down before the battle was over. As its bearers fell, the flag had been passed along the line until it had come into the hands of one of my privates, Joseph Collins, who carried it the remainder of the day. The color-bearers of the enemy had been even more unfortunate. On our charge into the corn-field, our men picked up several of their banners that had fallen with their bearers.

When night at length put a merciful end to the battle, all along the line, both thoroughly-worn-out armies were, I am sure, glad for the chance to rest. I know that I, for one, was completely exhausted. The sun had scarcely set before I had wrapped myself in my overcoat, and with my haversack for a pillow, was sound asleep, quite oblivious of the fact that the field of the dead was only a few steps away. In the morning we were early astir expecting a renewal of the fight. Our men threw away all of their old muskets, and armed themselves with the new Springfield rifles of the improved pattern, picked up on the battle-field. Ammunition and rations were issued, and every preparation made to receive the enemy. All was quiet, however, and so remained for the rest of the day. At about noon, General Franklin's Corps came up from Harpers Ferry and took position on our right.

During that afternoon I went over the corn-field that had been the scene of the hardest fighting the previous day. It was a sight which once seen could never be forgotten. The dead lay as they had fallen, and in such dreadful numbers! Several times had the ground been fought over; the bodies of brave men were so thickly strewn over it, that one might for rods have walked on corpses without touching the ground.

When we advanced our lines, the morning of the 19th, the enemy had disappeared. Only his picket line still remained, and that surrendered without resistance. These prisoners appeared to be dazed with discouragement; many of them seemed glad to have been taken. Like the thousands whom we had captured during the heat of the battle, they were destitute of clothing, and their haversacks contained nothing but raw corn.

In Winter Quarters

So far as we were concerned, the battle of Antietam ended active campaigning for the winter of 1862. During the next two months we moved about between Harpers Ferry and the mouth of Antietam Creek, doing occasional guard duty, and for the most part passing the time uneventfully. On October 1 President Lincoln visited our camp at Maryland Heights. It seemed to me that he did full justice to his reputation for homeliness. He came entirely unannounced, but we hurriedly turned out the Regiment and presented arms. For a time, on account of their greenness, the new regiments in camp furnished a source of amusement. Most of them had received large bounties on enlistment, and the old soldiers taunted them as bounty-bought; they were told that the Government could have secured mules much cheaper.

On November 13 came my commission as First Lieutenant of Company E. This did not materially change my position, for I had been in command of a company ever since the battle of Antietam. On November 17 we went into winter camp at Fairfax Station, but sometime in January removed to Stafford Court House. In the meantime McClellan had been finally removed from the command of the Army of the Potomac; and Burnside, who had followed him, had in his turn, been relieved after the battle of Fredericksburg, by General Joe Hooker.

Hooker was evidently determined to build up a thoroughly efficient army, and spent the winter in constant efforts toward improving the condition and effectiveness of his troops. Inspections became extremely rigid; they extended not only to arms and equipment, but to camp and garrison equipage, policing, and sanitation. Regiments reaching the highest standard for general efficiency and appearance were awarded leaves of absence for two officers at a time for fifteen days each, and furloughs for two men at a time, in each company, for the same period. Regiments that at first were not up to standard, were in the course of the winter given their furloughs as they attained efficiency.

Our Regiment was one of the eleven in the entire army which, when the first inspection was made, proved to be in the highest degree of efficiency. Leaves of absence and furloughs commenced at once, and before spring all who cared to go had a chance to visit their homes. The distance to Wisconsin was too great to make it profitable for me to return; so I visited a sister in New York State, taking advantage of this opportunity to see the sights of New York City and Washington.

During the winter the army was gradually strengthened by the return of convalescents. Thus our Regiment was able by spring once more to muster about 400 muskets. Many of the permanently disabled officers were transferred to the invalid corps, and those who were sick were discharged, thus giving way to more vigorous and able-bodied men. The army was now in the best condition that it had ever been in, and we all looked forward to a successful campaign.

Chancellorsville

On the morning of April 27, 1863, we left our winter camp at Stafford Court House and marched to Kelly's Ford on the Rappahannock. Pontoon bridges had been laid ahead of us, and the Eleventh Corps had already crossed. Early on the morning of the 29th, we followed, and started at once for Germanna Ford on the Rapidan, twelve miles off. Three corps of the Army of the Potomac were engaged in the expedition—the Fifth, Eleventh and Twelfth. Our Corps, the Twelfth, after crossing, pushed on to the head of the column, and our Brigade was given the position of honor in the advance. We carried eight days' rations and a hundred rounds of ammunition. In addition, several pack mules laden with boxes of cartridges followed each regiment, so that we felt sure we were out for business. The men were in good spirits, however, and notwithstanding the heavy loads marched rapidly.

We arrived at the ford in about four hours, without alarming the enemy. A portion of the Regiment were deployed as skirmishers under cover of the woods, three or four hundred yards from the river bank. At the word of command they moved on the run down to the river. Here each man hastily found for himself such shelter as he could, behind trees and brush, and opened fire on the enemy who were occupying some buildings on the opposite side. As we approached the river about a dozen Confederates started to run up the hill back of their position, in an attempt to escape. Our men were excellent marksmen, however, and after two had been killed and several others wounded, the rest of the enemy hastened back to the shelter of the buildings. Occasionally some fellow would fire at us from a window, but the puff of smoke from his gun would make him immediately the target for every musket within range, and that practice was soon discouraged. In less than ten minutes from the time when the skirmish commenced, the Southerners had hung out a white rag and surrendered. The swift-flowing Rapidan, nearly three hundred feet wide, separated them from us, but we compelled them to wade over. In this way, without a casualty to ourselves, we bagged 101 prisoners, and not a man escaped to the enemy to give warning of our approach.

We had just secured our prisoners when General Slocum came up. He immediately took in the situation, and ordered us to cross the river and secure the heights on the other side. We had had a good time laughing at our prisoners as we made them cross over to us, with the water up to their armpits; but when we had to go in ourselves, it did not seem so funny. It was still early in the spring, and the water was icy cold from the melting snow in the mountains. Moreover, the current was so swift that some mounted officers and cavalry who went in ahead of us could scarcely keep a footing. If a horse stumbled, he was washed off his feet in an instant and carried down stream. In fact, one man was drowned in such an accident, and several others had narrow escapes. We prepared for crossing by placing our ammunition and provisions, and such valuables as would be injured by the water, on the ends of the muskets or on our heads, and plunged in. We had the small men distributed among the large ones, and in this way crossed without serious trouble. We were followed in the same manner by the Second Massachusetts. Once across we pushed rapidly for the hill overlooking the ford, where we took a strong position and threw out our pickets.

The pontoon train had by this time come up, and a bridge was soon built. The remainder of our Corps and the Eleventh Corps then crossed and went into camp ahead of us. We now gathered about our fires, and dried out our clothes in order to have them once more in comfortable shape by bed-time.

The next morning we moved to Chancellorsville, where we arrived early in the day. It is a very big name for a very small place; at that time it contained only one house. The position which we had thus gained uncovered the road to United States Ford, on the Rappahannock. Here another pontoon bridge was laid, and General Hooker crossed it with his force. We were all in the best of spirits, for in securing this advantage of position we thought that the victory had already been gained.

On the morning of May 1 our Brigade engaged in a successful reconnoissance toward Fredericksburg, in which we captured a number of prisoners. On our return to Chancellorsville we were sent to occupy a slight rise of ground at Hazel Grove, about a mile southwest of Chancellor House. Here, in a sharp skirmish with the enemy, Lieutenant-Colonel Scott was shot through the head by a chance ball and instantly killed. During the afternoon, General Hooker rode around the lines, jubilant over the success of his movements. Several times he remarked that now he had got the Confederates where he wanted them, and they would have to fight us on our own ground or be destroyed. At that time the army still had unbounded confidence in him; but it seemed to me a bit curious that the man who was ready at Antietam to lead 150 men to a charge on the whole Southern army, should now get into entrenchment when he had at his command 150,000 soldiers.

The night passed off without incident. At about ten o'clock the next morning it was discovered that the enemy were moving wagon trains toward the southwest. Birney's Division of the Fifth Corps, which had been in position somewhere in our rear, was sent out at about noon to stop them. A sharp musketry fire for a minute or two indicated to us that the attack had been made, and soon after several hundred Southern prisoners were sent back to us under guard. At about four in the afternoon, our Regiment was ordered to deploy as skirmishers through the woods upon the left of Birney, to capture Confederate stragglers who were believed to be lurking there in large numbers. Obedient to these orders we piled up our knapsacks, overcoats, and other baggage, behind the breastworks we had built, and moved forward into the woods. We had advanced about half a mile from our entrenchments, when the storm broke loose in the rear. The army of Stonewall Jackson had struck the Eleventh Corps in the flank and rear, and had brushed it away like a swarm of flies before a hurricane. I was afterward told that the defeated Corps came tumbling along through the woods, an indiscriminate mass of flying men, pack mules with their packs turned, and stray artillery horses. Nor did they bring up until they were stopped at Chancellorsville by three regiments of Hooker's cavalry. However, the best troops in the world could not, if struck in the same way, have stood against such an attack.

Our line was now halted to await developments. Very soon a Confederate battery was in position on the hill which we had just left, and was throwing shells over toward Chancellor House. Directly in our front, to the south, another battery was firing in the same direction. We were hidden from this second battery by timber and underbrush, but were so close to it that in the intervals of the firing we could distinctly hear the strokes of swabs and rammers as the guns were swabbed out, and the charges rammed home. From my position I could see the battery near our old entrenchments, as it came up and commenced firing. However, it did not remain there long. The fire from our own batteries, near the Chancellor House, blew up two caissons or their limber chests, and the rest of the Southern battery sought a safer place.

The roar of artillery and musketry still continued around the Chancellor House and to the west of it; but we could tell by the sound of the firing that the Confederate advance had been stayed. By seven o'clock darkness had settled over the field, bringing with it for a time comparative quiet. We began to look around now, for a way out of the woods, and back to our Corps. Our scouts soon found that Geary's Division still held the entrenchments which they had built the night before, and that we might return safely through their lines to the Chancellor House. By nine o'clock, therefore, we were once more in line of battle with the rest of the Brigade, in the woods west of the House.

Shortly after our return, occurred the confusion in which Stonewall Jackson was mortally wounded. Our picket line had been driven in by the enemy, and we had fired a volley or two into the woods on our front. At the same time we had been fired on in the darkness by the Thirteenth New Jersey. General Jackson was struck just at this time, in the woods into which we had fired. It has been presumed that he was hit by his own men, but there is a possibility that the bullet came from the Third Wisconsin.

We secured but little sleep that night. Our artillery continued throwing shot and shell over our heads into the woods fronting us, where the enemy were supposed to be in force. At midnight the Confederates again attacked us; but Birney's Division, which had been cut off from us in the afternoon by Jackson's attack, struck them with fixed bayonets in the flank at the same time that we opened on them in the front—and of course we made short work of them. We had now regained the ground where we had left our knapsacks, but for fear of another attack, the officers would not let us go up after them. So we shivered miserably through the night, and in the morning arose thoroughly chilled.

The enemy, however, soon gave us enough to do to warm our blood. Birney's Division had, during the night, taken a new position in our advance, at Hazel Grove. It was attacked early Sunday morning, and in the course of an hour driven back with the reported loss of one of its batteries. As Birney's men passed back over us, the enemy came on, flushed with victory, and in some disorder. But in a few minutes we sent them back, in worse disorder than they had come. We followed them for a quarter of a mile, but there encountered a second line. In a short time we had the satisfaction of seeing their backs, also, dimly in the distance. Colonel Colgrove of the Twenty-Seventh Indiana, who was commanding the Brigade, now ordered a bayonet charge; but before we were fairly started, General Ruger sent orders not to advance any farther. Soon the enemy attacked again; but after a stubborn fight we sent them back for a third time, their ranks disorganized and the ground thickly strewn with their dead.

It was now near nine o'clock. We had been fighting continuously for three hours, and all of the ammunition that we carried had been exhausted. That carried by the pack mules had been distributed, also, and was nearly all fired away. The muskets had become so heated and foul that it was difficult to load them. Some of the pieces were so hot that the cartridge would explode as soon as it struck the bottom of the gun, and before the man had been able to aim. Because of this, we were relieved by a fresh brigade, and marched back about a mile to the rear. From there we were sent to a position a little northeast of the Chancellor House, where we built breastworks and remained until the army was withdrawn across the river.

All the rest of the day we could hear the firing to our right, and the next day, off in the direction of Fredericksburg, where Sedgwick's Corps was engaged; but we made no move. We only sat around, wearily watching the time pass away, until the night of the 5th, when preparations began to be made for the withdrawal of the army to the north bank of the river. The night was cold and rainy. Our blankets and overcoats had been lost, for we had left them on the second night of the battle to pick up stragglers, and fires were not permitted, lest they reveal our movement. As we shivered through the long, dark hours, all the admiration vanished that we had previously felt for Fighting Joe Hooker.

Toward day we silently withdrew from the entrenchments we had made, and marched off to the river. We found when we came near, however, that the approaches to the bridge were still crowded with the moving troops; we had, therefore, to double-quick back to the entrenchments, and wait until the bridge was cleared. Then we crossed over, the last of the army, entirely unmolested except for a few shells thrown by a Confederate battery.

We now returned to Stafford Court House, and at night pitched our tents on the very ground we had left ten days before. We were all thoroughly discouraged over the outcome of our expedition, and feeling, as one of our officers expressed it, "that we had gone out for wool, and come back shorn." The old soldiers who took part in that movement cannot think of it, to this day, but with the strongest feelings of disgust.

The camp that we occupied on our return to Stafford Court House was one of the best we ever had. It was an old orchard, with a vacant field near by for a drill and parade ground. Our friends, the Second Massachusetts, occupied one end of the orchard and we the other. Between us was a good baseball ground, where we amused ourselves at playing ball or pitching quoits. Every night after supper, the officers of the two regiments would get together for a big game, while the rank and file would follow suit, and our drill ground would present an animated sight. Thus we whiled away the time with considerable comfort, often speculating on the possibility of the enemy coming across the river to attack us. So many regiments of two-year men and nine-months men were being mustered out of the service, that we did not consider it at all likely that we would cross the river until our ranks were filled by the conscription which had then been ordered.

A Cavalry Expedition

On June 6 this easy life came to an end. The company commanders of our Regiment were summoned to the Colonel's tent, and informed that the Regiment had been selected to accompany a cavalry expedition. We were instructed to leave behind all baggage not carried on the persons of the men, and to take only those who could march thirty miles a day. The expedition was to be composed of the two best regiments in each corps—the Second Massachusetts and ourselves having been selected from the Twelfth.

We left our camp at about six o'clock and marched that night to Spott Tavern, fifteen miles away. The next day we reached Bealeton Station, where we bivouacked in the woods until the night of the 8th, awaiting the arrival of our cavalry. We were joined here by a number of other regiments, the whole force being under command of General Ames. Our State pride was highly gratified to find four Wisconsin regiments in this detail of picked commands from every corps.

On the night of the 8th, our whole force, infantry, artillery, and cavalry, moved down to the Rappahannock at Beverly Ford. The next morning, a portion of the Third Wisconsin was deployed to cover the crossing; but the enemy had not discovered us, and we passed over without trouble. The cavalry now pushed on to Brandy Station, on the railroad; the infantry following, with our detachment in the lead. The cavalry were soon briskly engaged, and in a little while Colonel Davis, their commanding officer, was brought back mortally wounded. The infantry was now disposed on the flanks, to guard the cavalry from being taken at a disadvantage. The fighting soon became general, being mostly by detached companies deployed as skirmishers. At one time, in advancing with my Company to clear out a piece of woods, I had a lively fight for a short time; five men out of the twenty with me were severely wounded before we drove the enemy from their shelter. At another time, Company D succeeded in getting on the flank and rear of a North Carolina regiment, and captured over a hundred prisoners. Some of our cavalry regiments were pretty severely handled at the beginning of the fight, especially before the infantry came up. On the whole, however, the expedition was a success, resulting in the capture of the headquarters of the Confederate cavalry leader, General J. E. B. Stuart, together with many valuable papers and orders relating to the contemplated invasion of the North.

Gettysburg

We now recrossed Beverly Ford and went into camp until the 12th. Then we learned that the Confederate army was on the move toward the North, and that our army was marching to Manassas Junction and Centerville. We therefore marched in the same direction, and on the 16th rejoined our Corps near Centerville. Reaching Leesburg on the 18th, we went into camp. We had no definite information as to the location of the Confederate army, but rather suspected that it was moving into the Shenandoah Valley. This suspicion was confirmed when we learned that they had occupied Winchester and Martinsburg. We heard of them next as crossing the Potomac at Williamsport and marching into Pennsylvania.

During our stay at Leesburg, several men from a New York regiment were shot for desertion. They were the first executions for that crime in our army, and for a time, they produced a great sensation. On the 26th we crossed the Potomac at Edward's Ferry, and proceeded up the river to the mouth of the Monocacy; thence we moved across to Frederick City, where we went into camp early on the afternoon of the 28th.

During the night I learned that our Division was under marching orders to strike for Williamsport in the morning, and destroy the bridge on which the enemy had crossed the Potomac. We were to destroy, also, all boats and ferries that might be used by the Confederates in a retreat. Then we were to rejoin the army if we could; if not, to move west to Cumberland, and rejoin as opportunity offered. With morning, however, came a change of commanders, and with it also, a change of orders. General Hooker had been superseded by General Meade, and now we were ordered northward to follow the army that had gone ahead.

At noon on July 1, while we were preparing our dinner at Two Taverns, some eight miles south of Gettysburg, the distant rumbling of artillery to the north announced to us the opening of a great battle. The cannonading became more and more furious as the minutes passed, until in the distance it sounded like one continual roll of thunder. At length came the order to march, and in five minutes we were on the road to the front as fast as our strength could take us. As we trudged along, we met hundreds of Confederate prisoners being sent to the rear, as well as a good many of our own wounded, on their way to the field hospitals. Of stragglers, there were exceptionally few.

On the run we reached Cemetery Ridge, where we learned that the First and Eleventh corps had been compelled to fall back through the town of Gettysburg. They had taken a new position on a ridge east of the city. A portion of our Brigade now filed off to the right, across Rock Creek, thence north about half a mile; and then, having deployed about half of our Regiment as skirmishers, advanced toward the west until we were sharply engaged with the enemy's skirmishers. Only a little over two hours had passed from the time when we received the order to march eight miles distant, before we were in position on the extreme right of the line of battle, checking the advance of the enemy in that direction. There we remained until sunset, when we were relieved by the cavalry, and recrossed Rock Creek to the west side.

As the remainder of our Corps had come up, they took position on the right of the First Corps. We now rejoined them there, our own right resting on Rock Creek. Immediately we began to throw up breastworks, and by evening had built for ourselves quite respectable entrenchments. It rained during most of the night; but in spite of that and the enemy, we secured a good rest for the next day's work.

Early the next morning we were stirring, in anticipation of an attack; but until noon there was nothing but skirmishing in our vicinity. Then the storm broke loose on the extreme left of the line, near Little Round Top, where Sickles's Corps was situated. The place was entirely hidden from our sight, and from the sounds we could form no opinion as to how things were going; but we were constantly receiving reports that Sickles was either holding his own or driving the enemy before him. In the light of subsequent events, these reports seem to have been purposely colored, in order to keep up our spirits. Occasional demonstrations along our front kept us in constant expectation of being attacked, but nothing of the sort occurred.

About six o'clock we were hurried out of our entrenchments at a double-quick toward Little Round Top, where it was understood that Sickles's Third Corps had been driven back with severe loss. But before we arrived, the enemy had been repulsed, and the firing ceased. We were now started back to our entrenchments. We found, however, upon our arrival, that the enemy had in our absence taken possession of them. It was exasperating to see them benefitting by our labors, but we were somewhat consoled by the capture of a picket of twenty Confederates, who in the darkness had wandered into our line as we approached. We were now obliged to form a new line, connecting with our forces on the left as before, but swinging back at an angle on the right to Rock Creek. We thus presented to the enemy a semi-circular front, which they could not penetrate without being subjected to a cross fire from both sides.

During the night we remained unmolested. At daylight the firing commenced. The ground occupied by the enemy's skirmishers was a rocky bit of woodland which furnished abundant cover for sharpshooters. For a while they annoyed us, but by nine o'clock we had dislodged them, and driven them back to the cover of their breastworks. On our left the enemy were making desperate efforts to dislodge from their entrenchments Greene's Brigade and the troops of the First Corps. Six times they came up to the assault, and six times were repulsed, leaving the ground over which they advanced literally covered with their dead. At about eleven o'clock a portion of our Division followed up these successes by charging the Confederates in our front and sweeping them entirely out of our entrenchments. They retired only a short distance, however, showing that they had not abandoned the contest.

For nearly two hours, complete quiet now succeeded the roar and din of the battle. Not a cannon was fired. Only an occasional musket shot disturbed the silence that prevailed from one end of the field to the other. We all felt, however, that this was but a lull before the final burst of the storm. The losses in our Regiment had thus far been light, and our spirits ran high. We felt entire confidence that no force that the Southerners could bring against us could by direct assault break our line at any point.

About one o'clock, the first shot was fired in the tremendous artillery duel that preceded the last desperate attempt to penetrate our center at Cemetery Ridge. In five minutes three hundred guns were pouring into one another, their deadly showers of shot and shell, and making fearful havoc of every thing that was not sheltered. From our position in the woods we could see nothing of what was going on in other parts of the line; but the air above was filled with screaming shells, as they flew back and forth on their deadly errand. In some instances, shells from the Confederate batteries in front of the Second Corps would pass entirely over our lines, and land near the enemy in our front; a great many of them fell in the open space in our rear.

At one time during the progress of the cannonade, a battery was placed in position on a hill across Rock Creek directly in front of our Regiment, and began to drop shells unpleasantly close to us. But our friends of Battery M, of the First New York Artillery, who had been with us since the Brigade was organized, seemed to get their range at once, and promptly silenced them. On a trip over the field, the next day, I found the position where they had been stationed marked by a dozen dead horses and two exploded caissons.

During the cannonading, I took occasion to go back into the woods a short distance in order to get a view of what was going on. Everything in sight gave evidence of the severity of the fire. All those who were not actively engaged had sought the shelter of rocks and trees or the inequalities of the ground. Here and there mounted officers and orderlies were riding across the field, although at first sight it seemed as though a bird could scarcely fly over it unharmed.

In the course of an hour the terrific artillery fire slackened. Then for a few minutes it nearly ceased. In the interval of silence, Pickett's Division of Confederates was marching to the charge. From my position I could not see them coming on, but I knew that they were charging by the old familiar Southern yell. Soon that was drowned in the roar of musketry and artillery.

For a time all was turmoil and confusion. At length the hearty cheers of our comrades rang out, and we knew that the Confederate tide of invasion had been safely rolled back.

While this assault was being made on the center, constant demonstrations were being made on our front, and we momentarily expected an attack. None came, however, although during all the rest of the day the enemy presented an unshaken line. At night they silently withdrew, and on the morning of the 4th our reconnoitering parties could find nothing of them east of Seminary Ridge, save their dead and severely wounded, whom they had left on the field.

I spent some time that day going over the ground occupied by the enemy in front of the Twelfth Corps, and that over which Pickett had made his now famous charge. From what I saw, I felt certain that the enemy's losses were double our own. Where they had assaulted Geary's Division on the evening of the 2nd and on the morning of the 3rd, the ground was so strewn with their dead that it would have been possible to walk for rods on dead bodies.

On the morning of the 5th the enemy was on the road back to Virginia. We started the same day following hard after them, on parallel roads to the east. When they reached Williamsport, however, they turned on us with a bold front. It had been raining almost constantly for several weeks and the Potomac was a raging torrent, which could not be forded. We were in hopes that it might thus continue until our forces could be concentrated to overwhelm them. On the morning of the 13th, however, when we were ready to move forward to the attack, they were gone. The river had fallen during the night, and they had made good their retreat.

For a time our Regiment led in the pursuit to the ford at Falling Waters. Then we were filed out to the side of the road to make way for General Kilpatrick's Cavalry Brigade. They had scarcely passed out of sight through a patch of woods, when the roar of artillery and the sharp crack of musketry announced that the enemy had been found. We moved forward as rapidly as possible, but were not in time to take any part in the conflict. It appeared that when the cavalry had emerged from the woods they had found a brigade of Confederate infantry posted as a rear guard, on a ridge overlooking the ford at Falling Waters. They had immediately charged the enemy's breastworks and had captured over a thousand prisoners. They had won, besides, as trophies of their skirmish, two pieces of artillery and four or five colors inscribed with all the battles of the Army of Northern

Virginia. No further pursuit was made. All of Lee's army, save only this rear guard, had escaped safely to the south side of the Potomac.

At about this time I sent to my home in Wisconsin the following letter concerning Lee's invasion:

> I have wished a good many times that the rebs could have had a month more among the people of Pennsylvania. What little sympathy I had for them is gone now. I cannot appreciate that disposition which will swindle a friend to compensate for what an enemy has stolen from you. In some cases the farmers would sell our men provisions at reasonable rates and even give them something, but the majority would ask from $.60 to $1.00 a loaf for bread, and $.25 a quart for milk, and all such things in proportion.

Our Corps now moved down the river to Harpers Ferry, and crossing into Virginia, marched leisurely along the eastern side of the Blue Ridge. We found the abandoned fields through which we passed overgrown with blackberry bushes, and literally black with the ripened fruit. Every night the men would go out from camp, and within easy range find as many berries as they could eat. And they were the best medicine we ever used. I knew of cases of diarrhea that had become almost chronic, soon cured by this diet.

On Draft Riot duty

On July 31 we went into camp near Kelly's Ferry on the Rappahannock, where for the next two weeks we did guard duty along the river and rested from the fatigue of the long marches we had made since leaving Stafford Court House. On August 15 came orders to move. The next morning we marched down to Rappahannock Station in company with two other old regiments of the Brigade, and boarded the cars for Alexandria, on our way to New York. We were joined at the station by five other regiments from the different brigades, all under command of General Ruger.

It seems that during the Confederate invasion of Pennsylvania, the New York militia regiments had been called off for duty in Washington, Baltimore, and other places. A riotous mob in New York City had taken advantage of this circumstance to break out in defiance of the authorities, and in resistance to the execution of the draft. They had for several days held the city in a reign of terror, and it had been necessary to stop all proceedings under the draft.

After a wait of several days, we embarked at Alexandria on the steamer "Merrimac," and proceeded down the Potomac to the ocean, thence to New York City. We landed at the foot of Canal Street, and quietly marched to the City Hall Park, where we arrived at about ten o'clock on Saturday night. Barracks had been provided for the enlisted men, but the officers' tents had not arrived. This did not trouble us much, however, as we had been without tents much of the time during the past two months. Wrapped in our rubber blankets, we lay on the grass and slept, as the landlady in *Rob Roy* says, "like a good sword in its scabbard." We awoke in the morning to find the sun well up in the heavens, and the park surrounded by a crowd of curious people, surprised to see a number of fairly well-dressed officers, sleeping on the ground like a lot of vagrants.

The next day, tents were pitched and cots prepared, and we were enjoying the delights of camp life amid all the surroundings of civilization. We had our dress parades and guard mountings with all the pomp and show that 300 men can make, to the delight of the great crowds who had come to see the veterans of Antietam and Gettysburg. Soon after our arrival I was detailed for duty in the provost marshal's office of the Fifth District of New York, where the rioting had been most desperate. I had charge of the guard stationed there to preserve order and see that those who brought substitutes or recruits were promptly admitted.

There were no disturbances in the city while we were there, except such as our men made for themselves, at the instigation of the police. We had plenty of bold fellows in the Regiment, who wanted no better amusement than to raid a saloon that had been the headquarters of the rioters. They would get out of camp at night, and gather in such a saloon pointed out to them by the police. Then they would get up a row on some pretext, and pitch bartenders and bummers out of doors, and smash everything breakable about the place. Everyone in the Regiment could find a way to enjoy himself, and a policeman to help him, and would have been content to stay in the city much longer than we did.

On September 6 came orders to return to our camp. We marched down to the Battery in the evening, and were conveyed in small boats to the steamer "Mississippi." In the morning, when I awoke, we were rolling and pitching in a manner that I had never before experienced in my limited travels by water. A few of the officers had become seasick on our way up to New York, and those of us who escaped had enjoyed the fun of laughing at them. I did not propose therefore to give up now. So I dressed and started for breakfast. One smell of the coffee, and I had business on deck. But after gazing steadily over the side of the vessel for a time, I felt better, and by noon had recovered my appetite.

We arrived at Alexandria on the 9th. On the 13th we reached our camp at Kelly's Ferry, and found the Thirteenth New Jersey drawn up in line to welcome us back to the old Brigade. We did not, however, remain long in camp. Rumors began to float about, that Lee was sending a part of his army to reënforce Bragg in northwestern Georgia. Within two days we were again on the march to the Rapidan, behind which the enemy had retired. We reached Raccoon Ford on the 16th, and our Regiment and the Second Massachusetts were detailed to support pickets at the Ford.

We camped in the woods near the river, with sentinels at night down to the bank, but during the day they were withdrawn to the most convenient cover in the neighborhood. The enemy were camped just behind the hills on the other side. Just about this time they appeared to be having a religious revival. While visiting my sentinels after dark, I could hear them preaching, praying, and singing, whole regiments apparently being thus engaged. Under orders from Corps headquarters we refrained from firing upon their pickets and they reciprocated the courtesy, which made it much pleasanter for the sentinels on both sides of the river.

With the Army of the Cumberland

After two days of this picket duty we were relieved by a Connecticut regiment and rejoined our Corps. We found that we were under orders to march the next day to Brandy Station, on the railroad. We did not know it at the time, but we were about to take our leave from the old Army of the Potomac, with which we had been associated since its organization. We had fought side by side in some of the hardest battles in the war; and had we been consulted in the matter, we would doubtless have voted to stay where we were, and help it to finish Lee's army. However, we were not consulted, and the necessities of war now called us to the Army of the Cumberland at Chattanooga.

On the night of the 24th, we bivouacked at Brandy Station, where the paymaster worked all night paying off the troops, and where we saw the Eleventh Corps being loaded for Alexandria. The next morning we marched to Bealeton Station, where, after a wait of a day, we also loaded up and started. The cars were ordinary freight trucks, with rough board benches set crosswise, and the men were crowded in as thick as they could be seated.

We pulled out of Washington over the Baltimore & Ohio Railroad, the trains containing forty or fifty cars each. As we approached the mountains the size of the trains was reduced to about seven cars; but on reaching the western slope, the old number was restored. We crossed the Ohio at Benwood, on a pontoon bridge. Another lot of cars was awaiting us on the opposite side, and we went on through Columbus, Dayton, Indianapolis, and Louisville. On this trip through Ohio and Indiana we were everywhere reminded that we were among friends. Our train stopped for a time at Columbus, Xenia, and Dayton, and it seemed as though the citizens of those towns could not do enough for us. At every station along the road great crowds of people were gathered, and cheered us as we passed along.

We stopped briefly at Louisville, then went on again through Nashville, and past the battle-field of Murfreesboro. We debarked from the cars at Stevenson, Alabama, on Sunday morning, just a week from the time we had started. We certainly were glad enough to be released after seven days and nights of railroad travelling, cramped up so tightly that there was scarce room either to sit up or lie down. Our arrival was none too soon. The long line of railroad from Nashville southward, had been practically unguarded, and the enemy's cavalry under General Wheeler succeeded soon after our arrival in tearing it up in several places.

We now had several weeks of racing up and down the railroad line, infantry after cavalry, and with the usual result. In the end, however, the road was cleared, with the whole "Red Star" Division distributed between Murfreesboro and Stevenson. Our Regiment was stationed at Wartrace, where there was a junction with a short railroad running to Shelbyville—the Nashville & Chattanooga Railroad. It was a curiosity. The cross-ties were about five feet apart, and the rails were of wood, surmounted by a running surface of light iron. Frequently the wooden rails would spread, and then there would be a wreck; in fact, scarcely a day passed on which there would not be an accident of some kind. Large details of men from our Regiment were set to work to bring the road in repair, and by Christmas it was in fairly good condition.

Shortly after we were established at Wartrace, I secured leave of absence to go to Chattanooga in search of my brother, who had enlisted in the Tenth Wisconsin. I had not heard of him since the battle of Chickamauga. My route was by rail to Bridgeport on the Tennessee River, then in a small captured Confederate steamer called "Paint Rock," up the Tennessee to Chattanooga.

The "Paint Rock" was loaded to its utmost capacity with hardtack for the starving Union men who held Chattanooga. The river route to that town had only recently been opened up by General Hooker, with the Eleventh Corps and the Second Division of our Corps. Previously it had been necessary to wheel all supplies sixty miles over a mountain road, where teams could scarcely haul the forage for their own trip. Even now the boats could run only to within eight miles of the city.

The fifty-mile river trip brought me at the end of the day to the landing at Kelly's Ferry. Then I had an eight-mile walk before me to the camps, where I arrived late in the evening. I soon found the regiment or the small remnant of it that I was looking for; but then I learned that my brother was beyond doubt a prisoner in the hands of the enemy.

I spent a day in visiting about Chattanooga. The enemy occupied a line from the Tennessee River, above town, to the point of Lookout Mountain below. At no place were they near enough to throw shells into the city, save from their heavy guns on Lookout Mountain. From these, shells came over all day at intervals of ten or fifteen minutes and exploded high in the air over either our camps or the city. So far as I could see, however, they did little damage.

Shortly after my return to my Regiment, I was detailed to investigate the killing of a negro by a white man, not far from our post. The evidence showed that it was a most unprovoked murder, and I so reported. The man was thereupon arrested and sent to the provost marshal at Tullahoma. I never learned what was finally done with him. The curious thing about the affair was the frank astonishment of the man that anyone should take notice of the killing of a mere "nigger."

Toward the end of November a large number of Confederate prisoners, who had been captured in the battles of Lookout Mountain and Missionary Ridge, were being sent northward over the railroad. We often had conversation with them while the trains were stopping at our station. Some were still defiant, but most of them were discouraged, and many predicted that the Confederacy could not last six months longer. An unusually large number of deserters of all ranks from colonel downward, were also coming in, and they likewise professed to believe that the Confederacy was tottering.

The Third Veteranizes

In December a general order was issued from the War Department, providing for the reënlistment of veteran regiments. It provided for a liberal bounty for all who reënlisted as veterans after two years' service; but it offered what was a greater temptation than anything else, the chance to go home for thirty days as a regiment, with the opportunity to recruit up to the full standard. I explained to my Company all the advantages of this arrangement. Their term of service would not expire until the end of June. By that time the fighting would probably be well over with. By reënlisting now they would secure the bounty, the thirty days furlough, and the honorable record of veteran soldiers, and it would be possible to preserve our organization from the beginning to the end of the war.

Just about this time I was called away from camp to Tullahoma, to sit on the court martial of Colonel E. L. Price of the One Hundred Forty-Fifth New York Regiment, on charges of misbehaviour in battle. When the court adjourned over the Christmas holidays and I returned to my Regiment, I was informed by my First Sergeant that the men of my Company had been talking over the matter of reënlisting, and that more than three-fourths of them were ready to do so if I would stay with them. The contagion spread. By Christmas all but two of the officers, and 240 out of 300 enlisted men present with the Regiment, had, in the language of the day, "veteranized."

On Christmas this surviving remnant of the thousand men of the Third, who had so gayly left the State two-and-a-half years before, started on their return. It was a beautiful day, and for us one of perfect happiness. We were going home with a record that none could surpass and few commands could equal. We were the first regiment from Wisconsin, and I believe the first in the army, to reënlist.

At Madison the arms were stored, and the men scattered to their homes to enjoy their thirty-days' furlough. I was just in time to take part in a New Year's dance, and go home in the morning on the coldest day ever known in Wisconsin.

The month of January, 1864, which we spent in Wisconsin, was a season of continuous festivities. The only drawback was the extreme cold, which to us who had just come from the South, seemed more severe than it had ever been before. Everyone seemed to be determined to give the returned soldiers the best time of their lives. Some of the croakers thought it too gay for people who were engaged in a death struggle for the life of the Nation. Those of us, however, who had been at the front, were disposed to be merry while we could, and leave the future to care for itself. Recruiting was going on all the time. Our veterans proved the best recruiting officers in the State. They brought in their brothers and cousins, schoolmates and friends, so that when we were ready to return once more to the south, we had added 300 men to our rolls, picked from the very flower of Wisconsin's citizenry.

On February 2 the veterans of the Regiment assembled at Madison. On the 4th we were again on our way south, and reached Tullahoma the night of the 9th. On the 12th we started out for Fayetteville, the seat of Lincoln County, Tennessee, where we arrived at noon on the following day. On our way we passed through Lynchburg, where there was pointed out to us the house, or rather the ruins of the house, which was said to have been the birthplace of Davy Crockett. At Mulberry, a little farther on, I met a middle-aged citizen who said that he had never known what a United States flag looked like until he had seen one carried by our soldiers in this war.

Reorganizing Lincoln County

Lincoln County was one of the richest, as well as the most violent of Secession counties in Tennessee. Its people boasted that it had cast 2,500 votes for Secession, and not one for the Union; the few Union men in the county had not dared to go to the polls. A few months previous to our coming a small detachment of Northern troops had been captured there by guerrillas. The prisoners had been taken to the bank of the Elk River and three of them deliberately murdered. A fourth had only escaped by leaping into the river and swimming off in the confusion. When he had reported the matter to headquarters, Colonel Ketcham of the One Hundred Fiftieth New York had been sent to collect an assessment of $30,000 from the citizens of the county for the benefit of the families of the murdered soldiers.

Our mission in Lincoln County was to hunt down the guerrillas who infested it, and to care for the refugees from Chattanooga and other places in the rear of the army, who had lost their means of gaining a livelihood. We supported the refugees by forced levies of corn and bacon from the wealthy planters of the vicinity, while our mounted force soon disposed of the guerrillas, capturing a number and frightening the rest out of the county. We had a novel way of administering justice. For instance, about two months after our arrival a number of these young offenders, whose parents lived in the vicinity and were substantial farmers, stole from a citizen mules valued at $400. The Colonel immediately assessed the amount on the fathers, and with the money thus collected paid for the mules. That was our policy all through—to make the wealthy Confederates pay for the damage done by their lawless colleagues. And this method had a good effect, for it soon put an end to the thievery.

Shortly after we arrived, our mounted men captured a Confederate officer named Boone, a grandson of the famous Daniel. On him was found a list of all the guerrillas in the county. When I examined him, he told me that he had been sent to muster these fellows into the Confederate army; but his plans were spoiled. Instead he went to Johnson's Island, a prisoner, and his little memorandum book remained in my possession.

Among the names on the list were those of two Miller boys, whose mother and sister lived in town. The Captain of our mounted men, and several other officers, boarded with the family, for the people in Fayetteville were usually glad to take in Union officers as boarders, in order that they might secure from our rations the otherwise unobtainable luxuries of sugar and coffee. Several days after the capture of Boone's list, the Captain brought in both of the young Millers as prisoners. They were forwarded to Corps headquarters at Tullahoma. The elder, instead of being sent North as a prisoner of war, was tried by court martial and sentenced to be hanged in the public square of Fayetteville. That did not suit some of us; so we found means to send Mrs. Miller to Shelbyville, where she secured Judge Cooper, a well-known Unionist and former member of Congress, to go to Washington, and lay the case before President Lincoln. It was well known that no death sentence was ever executed with the President's consent, if there was any reasonable excuse for avoiding it. His usual magnanimity did not fail in this case, and the boy was sent North as an ordinary prisoner of war.

When the President's amnesty proclamation was issued, we were given the duty of reorganizing Lincoln County under its provisions. I was appointed provost marshal, and in that position administered oaths of allegiance to several thousand repentant and unrepentant Secessionists. When the election was held, returns were made to me, and by me tabulated, and sent to the military governor at Nashville. Commissions were then issued by him to the officials who had been elected, so that when we left, the county was ready to resume civil government.

In administering the oath of allegiance, the demand for blanks was so great that the ordinary sources could not furnish a sufficient supply. It was necessary, therefore, for me to open a printing office. So I took possession of an old printing establishment, and set several men to work. The press was broken down and the type badly "pi'd"; but we soon had the machinery repaired, and by combining the stock of three printing offices, secured sufficient type to run our establishment with success.

In addition to these other duties, I had to listen to everyone in the county who sought redress for a grievance of any kind. Some had had horses taken by our army, or by bushwhackers; some had been robbed of money or other valuables; some wanted permits to carry firearms, which were of course never granted; and others needed assistance from the Government to keep from starving. One man came with a case parallel to that of the woman who wanted a "pass to raise geese." He wanted a "pass to raise a crup." I told him to go on and raise his crop, or do whatever he pleased, so long as he remained loyal to the Government. He said his neighbors had told him he could not raise a crop without a permit from the Federals, and that every man who took the oath of allegiance was branded in the forehead with the letters "U. S."

One day a woman came to me, who said she had heard that we paid $10,000 to the widows of men killed by guerrillas. I explained to her that we had done that only for the widows of three Union soldiers. I told her, however, that if she could give me any information about where the guerrillas could be found, we would capture and punish them. She said she did not know, but that she had heard some shots in the woods. She had not seen her man since, and she was sure they had killed him. After parleying awhile she started out of the door. But before she went out, she turned and called back to me, "That ai'nt the wust of 't; they stole my old mare, too!"

When we first arrived at Fayetteville not a person was to be seen on the streets, although before the war it had been a place of 2,000 inhabitants. There was not a vestige of any kind of business left in the town. Even the stores and taverns were vacant. The people soon made their appearance, however, when they found that we had come to stay, and before very long we had established the most friendly relations with them. By the time we were ready to leave, almost every family in town had its friends among the soldiers. They were very sociable, and always seemed glad to have the Federal officers call on them. The young ladies would sing and play the piano beautifully, and make things quite homelike for us after the routine of the day's work. Twenty years later, while passing through Fayetteville on my way to Atlanta, I received courtesies from a citizen who only knew me by reputation as one of the officers of the Third Wisconsin.

It was curious to see what a difference slavery had made in the social life of these people. Everywhere work was considered disgraceful for a white man, and as only the occupation of the "nigger." In order to succeed socially, it was necessary to own slaves. The idea of hiring labor, or of being rich without negroes, was apparently incomprehensible. And in fact it was true that all of the people who had obtained any sort of success, intellectually or otherwise, had owned slaves.

Most of the men who resided in the vicinity had served in the Confederate army. Some had been discharged on account of wounds or sickness, while others, and probably most of them, had deserted when they became sure that the fight was hopeless.

My office was a common resort for these people after they had taken the oath of amnesty. They would sit around by the hour, and spin their yarns about the Confederate service. The recent deserters had to be sent to headquarters at Tullahoma for examination; and as we could communicate only with a strong escort, I would sometimes have half a dozen of them paroled to report to me daily until I could arrange to send on a party.

In all my dealings with these people, I found scarcely any who really desired the success of the Union cause. There were plenty of them, probably the majority, who thought the Confederacy a failure, and wished to get back into the Union on the best possible terms; but they still clung to their old ideas. However, that did not interfere with our friendship and the good time that we had while we were there. And when the day at length came when we were obliged to leave, I think that they really were, as they professed to be, sorry at our going. And well they might be, for the regiment of Tennessee Union Cavalry, that occupied the town after we left, proceeded at once to kill several of the most prominent men who had not taken the amnesty oath, and at least one who had.

On the morning of April 28, 1864, we said farewell to our Fayetteville friends and started out on the campaign which a year later was to end at Raleigh, North Carolina, with the surrender of Johnston's army and the end of the war. With us was a company of Tennessee Union Cavalry, commanded by Captain Brixey, which had been sent to Lincoln County to hunt bushwhackers. On leaving Fayetteville they had taken a horse belonging to Judge Chilcote, a prominent citizen, who had been of much assistance to me in the provost marshal's office in restoring civil government, and who had at the election been chosen county clerk. The Judge followed us, and asked to have his horse restored. Colonel Hawley of our Regiment at once compelled Captain Brixey to give it up. He did so with apparent reluctance, and then secretly sent a number of his men over a by-road to intercept the Judge on his return and kill him. This cowardly deed accomplished, the men rejoined their command. Brixey then pushed on ahead to Tullahoma, and on the next day left for the mountains of East Tennessee. The murder was reported to us that night. The Colonel sent back Captain Gardner with his mounted men to investigate, but the murderers had fled as soon as their deed became known, and nothing more could be done. After this outrage, Brixey never dared to rejoin our army. Some time later he was killed by Confederates in northwestern Georgia.

During our stay at Fayetteville our Corps and the old Eleventh of the Army of the Potomac were consolidated, and became known as the Twentieth Corps of the Army of the Cumberland. The command was given to General Hooker. Our portion of the army would very much have preferred General H. W. Slocum, who was sent to Vicksburg. In the reorganization we became the Second Brigade of the First Division, with General Thomas H. Ruger commanding the Brigade and General A. S. Williams commanding the Division. At the suggestion of the officers of the Eleventh Corps, our old badge, the five-pointed star, was retained as the badge of the new corps.

Opening of the Atlanta Campaign

Our Regiment reached Tullahoma on April 30, to find that the rest of our Brigade had already gone to the front. We started out on the next day to join them, and on May 4 crossed the Tennessee River at Bridgeport. On the 7th we passed over the battle-field of Chickamauga, where signs of the conflict were still everywhere in evidence. On the night of the 8th we crossed the mountains by way of Nickajack Pass, and joined our Brigade at daylight the next morning. This passage over the mountains was interesting. The night was extremely dark and perfectly quiet. The men in charge of the wagon train had placed lighted candles on the rocks along the road, at intervals of about a hundred feet, in order to guide themselves and those who came after. These were still flickering when we came along.

Our march to Atlanta was now well under way. The enemy continually fell back, and in most cases without offering serious resistance. The three armies of General Sherman, marching in parallel lines, seemed to be able to carry everything before them. On the 10th we again crossed the mountains at Snake Creek Gap, going into camp on the other side until the 13th. On the night of the 10th we were visited by a tremendous wind and rain storm, which blew down our tents, and raised the water in the creek so high that we had to move our camp or be drowned. At about this time, also, an order was read to the troops announcing the great success of the Army of the Potomac in the opening battles of the final campaign against Richmond.

On the 14th we were moved to the extreme left to support General Howard, who was there engaged with the enemy. We arrived at about sundown, just as the Confederates were driving in a brigade of the Fourth Corps and threatening to capture a battery of artillery. As we moved forward in line of battle, ready to receive the advancing enemy, General Williams called out to the fleeing soldiers of the Fourth Corps to get back out of the way, for he had a division there from the Army of the Potomac that would protect them. All of which goes to show that even major-generals are human, and when they get a chance like to exult over their rivals. We checked the advance of the enemy without much trouble.

At about noon on the 15th, General Butterfield, with our Third Division, moved forward to attack an earthwork and a four-gun battery, which the enemy held in his front. We moved forward on the left to support him; and encountering little opposition at first, advanced somewhat farther than the Third Division. We took position in the edge of a woods, where we made use of a rail fence and some logs to build a breastwork in anticipation of an attack, which the skirmish firing in front warned us was coming. We soon had sight of the advancing enemy. A few volleys from us, however, and they broke and ran. In a short time they again came up, with a new line. We disposed of that almost as quickly as the first. A third time they repeated the attempt, and again we beat them back.

Now came the order to pursue. My Company, and the companies on my right, moved forward about two hundred yards in the woods. Suddenly we found that we were on the flank of a Brigade that was still stubbornly fighting with troops of the Twenty-Third Corps and the left companies of our Regiment. They were in a peach orchard, the nearest of them not fifty yards away. I hastily wheeled my Company, and Company H to the left, and opened fire. At such short range, and in such a crowd, every shot must have counted. The Confederates did not wait for much, but skedaddled as fast as their legs could carry them.

Just as the last of them were disappearing from sight, I saw a man in Confederate uniform come running toward my Company, hatless, but with gun in hand. I supposed that he was coming in to give himself up. He came within twenty yards of us, then apparently noticed for the first time that we were Yankees. He immediately started to run back. I called to him to surrender, but it only increased his speed. Finding that he did not stop, two of my men fired at him, and both hit him. He fell dead almost instantly upon the field. I went forward then and examined him. He was a mere boy, not over twenty years of age. In his pocket we found his order, not two weeks old, from the conscript officer of his district, notifying him to join the army. I have seen fields of battle in front of our Regiment, covered over with the dead, without experiencing the pang of regret that I felt for this poor lad who, scarcely out from home, and too frightened and confused to know what to do, thus sadly met his fate.

The loss of our Regiment in this fight was one killed and thirty-one wounded. Many of the wounded subsequently died, among them Reverend John M. Springer, the Chaplain of the Regiment. When drafted in 1863, he had been a Methodist minister in Monroe, Wisconsin. Believing this to be a call of duty he had refused to allow his church to secure a substitute, and had reported at Madison for service. When our Regiment was about to leave Wisconsin for the front, after the veteran furlough, we officers had been introduced to him in the Executive Chamber at the Capitol, where we had assembled on the invitation of the Governor. When sent for, Springer had been found doing sentinel duty before the gate of Camp Randall. We had elected him Chaplain, and he had joined us at Fayetteville as soon as he could secure his discharge as a private. On the morning of the battle, when the prospects seemed good for a lively fight, he had come to me and asked for a musket and some ammunition, for he did not wish to be lurking in the rear while we were in danger at the front. At my suggestion, he had previously posted himself in the tactics, so I now told him to take the place of a Lieutenant in my Company. He was the first man hit, and died in the hospital a few days later.

By a strange coincidence, our picket found on the field in our front the dead body of the Chaplain of the Georgia Regiment with which we had been engaged. We were told by some of the wounded prisoners that he had been shot in coming up to recover the body of his son, a captain in the Regiment, who had been killed early in the fight.

In this battle, for the first time in my experience, Confederate soldiers who might have escaped came in and gave themselves up as prisoners. I think as many as forty did this. They were all thoroughly discouraged, and the same feeling seems to have run through their whole army, for they were more quickly and easily beaten than I had ever seen them before.

It was understood on our part that in order to give the Army of the Tennessee time to get below Resaca and cut off their retreat, we were not to push the attack against the enemy. They were too quick for us, however; the next morning they had abandoned Resaca, leaving behind them six heavy guns and large quantities of provisions and ammunition.

On the 19th we came up to them again at Cassville, where we drove them into their entrenched lines and occupied the town. We expected a fight in the morning, but once more they were gone, this time across the Etowah River. After a rest of four days at Cassville, we again went forward, crossing the Etowah on a pontoon bridge without resistance.

On the 25th we had nearly reached Dallas when we were turned back to assist General Geary, who had encountered a division of Hood's Corps, entrenched on the Marietta road to our left, at a place called New Hope Church. On our arrival we found that Geary's Division had already pushed back the enemy's skirmishers until the latter were thought to be in their main line of works, from which position we were ordered to drive them. The country was heavily timbered, and underbrush so obscured the view that it was impossible to see in any direction more than a few rods. When we came within sight of the enemy we found that a six-gun battery was posted a little in front of their line of infantry. The latter awaited us behind a breastwork, evidently hastily constructed of logs and earth, nevertheless affording fairly good shelter. As soon as we came within range, the battery opened on us with round shot and shell; then, as we came nearer, with grape and canister. But we pushed steadily on until we were less than sixty yards from them, when we halted; for we had lost so many men, and had become so disorganized in the march through the timber and brush that the impetus of our charge was gone. The regiments on both sides of us had already done the same. We sheltered ourselves as well as we could, behind trees and fallen timber, and opened fire on their battery, receiving a hot fire in return from their infantry. We succeeded, however, in driving off the Confederate gunners, and prevented the cannon from being worked for the remainder of the day.

Wounded and in Hospital

When we had first come within range of the grape-shot, my scabbard had been struck and cut in two at a point just below where I grasped it with my left hand. Later, when my men had sheltered themselves and had commenced firing, I was again struck. I was at the time resting on one knee in a position where I could watch the battery, and direct our fire upon it, for I was determined that the enemy should not have an opportunity to take it away so long as we had a chance to capture it. My attention had just been called to something on the left, when a bullet struck the front of my cap, cutting the figure "3" out of the bugle, and glancing from the bone, cut a gash across my forehead. For a time I lost all interest in that battle. When I regained my feet, Colonel Hawley, who was standing near, told me to get back to the hospital. I succeeded in finding my way to a small ravine that we had crossed, thinking as I got back of the line, that there were a thousand bullets flying, to every one nearer the front. At the small brook in the ravine, I tried to wash off the blood which was blinding me, but had such poor success that I concluded to follow the Colonel's advice and have the wound dressed. I considered it not much of a clip, and thought that in three days at the most I would be back with my company. It was about two months before I rejoined, and a good many years before I entirely recovered.

On my way back to the hospital, I met in succession General Williams who commanded the Division, General Hooker who commanded the Corps, General Thomas who commanded the Army of the Cumberland, and General Sherman who commanded the Department. Each stopped and asked if I was much hurt—when I told that it was only a scratch, they were eager for information as to the situation at the front. I explained that we had driven the artillerymen from their guns, but that the infantry in their breastworks had been too much for us. Then each kindly told me to go to the hospital.

At the hospital I found Dr. Conley, our Regimental Surgeon, who dressed my wound and gave me a blanket to lie down on. I got away to one side and tried to sleep, but the Doctor disturbed me so often to look at my wound that this was impossible. I finally lost all patience with him and ordered him to let me alone; but he afterwards explained that he feared I would go to sleep and wake up in the next world.

This fight is known in the North as the Battle of Dallas, or the Battle of Pumpkinvine Creek, and in the South as the Battle of New Hope Church. In the engagement, our Regiment lost eighteen men killed and ninety-two wounded. This loss was quite unevenly distributed among the companies. Mine had sixteen men severely wounded, two of whom subsequently died. Company A, on my left, had six men killed and twenty-one wounded. Captain Hunter of Company F was wounded by a canister shot, in one of his legs near the knee-joint, and died shortly after. Captain Ruger of the Brigade staff also received a severe wound in the knee, which incapacitated him for further service during the war.

On the afternoon of the day following the battle, I thought I was strong enough to go back to my Regiment. So I started out, against the protests of the surgeons; but after going about a quarter of a mile, my legs gave out, and I was obliged to return and obey directions. I remained at the field hospital for about three and a half days. During most of that time the surgeons were busy at the amputating table. On the morning of the 29th all of the slightly wounded were sent off with the wagon train. The more seriously wounded were sent off late in the afternoon in the ambulances. Captains Hunter, Ruger, and I went in the same ambulance, I was on the seat with the driver.

At Kingston, where we arrived on the 30th, a long train of freight cars for the slightly wounded, and hospitals cars for the severely wounded was waiting, ready to start for Chattanooga. Captain Hunter was, however, too ill to go, and I would not leave him, so we waited over together until June 2. The ride to Chattanooga was a very severe one for poor Hunter, and he appeared to be much the worse for it. He recovered temporarily under the careful treatment at Chattanooga, of Doctor Persons of the First Wisconsin Cavalry, but on June 8 began to sink rapidly, and died on the afternoon of the following day.

My wound was not dangerous, yet it was serious enough to entitle me to a leave of absence. I took advantage of it to return for a pleasant week to my Wisconsin home; then rejoined my Regiment near the Chattahoochee River on July 17. During my absence it had followed the fortunes of the Twentieth Corps, having had no hard fighting and but few casualties on the picket line.

The term of service of the men who had not reënlisted had expired on June 29, and they had been mustered out. The officers in the various regiments, however, who wished to be mustered out, found themselves conscripted for a longer term. Their applications had been approved until they had reached General Thomas; but he had forwarded them to Washington with recommendations for dishonorable discharge. Discovering this danger, the officers had withdrawn their applications. A number in the Twenty-Ninth Pennsylvania had, however, been dishonorably discharged under such circumstances, and at the time this seemed to us an injustice.

The Siege of Atlanta

On the day that I rejoined the Regiment the army moved forward across the Chattahoochee River. During the next three days a farther advance was made across Peach Tree Creek, and we were now but a few miles from the fortifications of Atlanta. On the afternoon of the 20th, General Hood, the new Confederate commander who had succeeded Johnston, came out of his entrenchments and made a furious attack on our lines. The brunt of it fell on our Corps, which was somewhat in advance of the others. Our Regiment being in the second line was not engaged, for the first line repulsed the enemy along the entire front. The fighting was very severe, the Confederates coming up to the attack again and again. The loss in our Corps was about 2,000 killed and wounded; that of the enemy must have been double that number.

On the night of the 21st I went on picket duty with instructions to advance my picket line if possible, for the enemy's pickets were so close that their stray bullets were causing much annoyance in our camp. We were not very successful during the night; but in the morning, when the whole Brigade picket line under Major Smith of the One Hundred Fiftieth New York, moved forward, the enemy had disappeared. As was now becoming quite usual, a number of their men remained behind to be taken prisoners.

Major Smith's orders were to advance until he found the enemy. So we slowly pushed forward through their strong but abandoned works, and encountered no serious opposition until within about a mile of their fortifications immediately surrounding the city. We met their picket line on a hill, and drove it back a half mile, but they brought out against us such a strong force that we in turn were obliged to fall back, taking our stand on the hills where we had first met their pickets. From this position they did not seriously attempt to dislodge us.

From our vantage we could see all of their manœuvers. Apparently there were not more than 2,000 or 3,000 troops to prevent our entry into the city. I have always believed that if there had been someone high enough in command to have used the troops where I was that day, Atlanta could have been captured much more easily than it was six weeks later. At about six o'clock our Corps came up, and our picket line, once more moving forward, drove the Confederate skirmishers to within two hundred yards of their forts.

The next day a battery of twenty-pound Parrott guns was planted on the hill and commenced throwing shells into the city over our heads. The enemy replied with spirit, and we received many of their compliments that were intended for the battery. Our men protected themselves by throwing up an earthwork in front of the camp, with a ditch behind it wide enough and deep enough to shelter all in case of necessity. The officers all had heavy earth barricades built in front of their tents, and these furnished fairly good protection.

I remember to have been one night in the Colonel's tent when the shells were flying pretty lively. We were just discussing whether his embankment would stop a shell, when one came along and buried itself in the ground a little in front without exploding. The Colonel went out and found that it had gone two feet into the ground. One of the other officers present expressed the opinion that it would have gone through the breastwork if it had struck properly. The words were scarcely out of his mouth when another shell struck the work, penetrating about two-thirds of the way, and exploding without damage.

At another time we were not so fortunate. A shell struck the barricade of Captain Orton of Company K, passed through, and exploded in the tent, mortally wounding him and seriously wounding Lieutenants Barager, Blanchard, and Schweers, who were with him. Lieutenant Barager served until the end of the war; but a few years after its close, he became, as a consequence of that shock, a physical and mental wreck.

The enemy's sharpshooters were close enough to us to keep dropping their bullets incessantly into our camp. It was at first rather annoying to have them come pattering around whenever anyone moved, but in time we became so accustomed to the missiles, that we went about our ordinary business as though there were no Confederates within forty miles. On one occasion the Thirteenth New Jersey went out in front of the line and captured thirty-five of the enemy's pickets, and burned the houses where the marksmen had been stationed.

On July 28 General Hooker was at his own request relieved of the command of our Corps. He had taken offence at being jumped by General Howard for the command of the Army of the Tennessee, after the death of

General McPherson in the battle of July 22. I do not believe that the highest officers generally sympathized with Hooker, but the Corps as a whole felt that his loss was a serious blow. He had large personal influence on his troops. During an active campaign, virtually every soldier in his Corps saw him almost daily. If there was a picket line to be established, he personally examined it; if an assault was made on the enemy, he was with the foremost, always brave to the extreme of recklessness. He was, moreover, careful of the welfare of his men. He made his commissaries attend strictly to business, and his Corps would often be furnished with the delicacies of army rations when others were short or had nothing but hardtack and salt pork. It was a common remark all through the army that Joe Hooker fed his men the best, and fought them the best, of any of the corps commanders. Of course his men worshipped him and under him were invincible; for the same reason the enemy dreaded him worse than anything else mortal.

The newspapers of the day said that the appointment of General Howard was the work of President Lincoln. But it was reported in the Corps, that General Sherman had been the prime mover. It was freely whispered among us that Sherman, with all his great talents and acknowledged ability, was affected with the same weakness that was said to have troubled Napoleon—the not being able to look with complacency on the great personal popularity of a subordinate. Sherman was reported to have allowed this feeling to break forth into positive insult of General Hooker and his Corps in the presence of subordinates. For instance, on the night after the battle of Peach Tree Creek, before any returns of casualties had been made, Hooker told Sherman that he had lost that day nearly 2,000 men. "Oh pshaw!" answered Sherman, "that's nothing; they'll all be back in the morning." Later it was found that 1,700 members of the Corps had been killed or wounded, and that they had successfully repulsed the whole Confederate army with a reported loss to the latter of 6,000.

Before leaving, General Hooker invited all the colonels in the Corps to call on him, and told them frankly his reasons for resigning. He said that during the whole campaign he had been subjected to unbearable insults and indignities, and his Corps and its performances had been underrated and disparaged. And now, to have promoted over him a junior officer from this Department, whose rank and service were far below his, was the last straw; his reputation as a soldier and his honor as a man would not, he said, admit of his remaining.

The enemy's picket line had been temporarily quieted by the advance of the Thirteenth New Jersey, but was now again annoying us. These pickets were on a ridge about two hundred yards in front of their main line of works, and not more than four hundred yards from our camp. They had lines of pits dug all along their position and could at any time communicate with their main line. Our pickets were also located in pits, but could only be relieved at night. It was determined to reverse this order of things. So at daylight on July 30, at a preconcerted signal, our whole Brigade picket line, under command of Lieutenant-Colonel Morse of the Second Massachusetts, jumped out of their pits, crossed the intervening space at a run, and captured the enemy's entire line, numbering seven officers and ninety-seven men.

A regiment was immediately sent out to reënforce our men, and breastworks were hastily thrown up. From their forts and main breastworks, the enemy poured into us a shower of shot and shell; but our men held their position all day, many of them firing as much as two hundred rounds of ammunition. At night the position was made impregnable against anything save a movement in large force; and in the morning the enemy were compelled to withdraw their artillery and close the embrasures of their forts.

For some weeks there was not much change in the situation, so far as we were concerned. There was much hard work for the men in the trenches, and they were all getting anxious for the capture of Atlanta. I believe nine-tenths of them would rather have fought the matter out in an open battle than to have kept on scraping and shoveling to dig them out. It seemed to us at the time that between our army and that of the Confederates, there had been enough dirt dug, from Louisville to Atlanta, to have built all the railroads in the United States.

For a time in our advanced position, firing on the picket line was constant, and there were many casualties. In a week or two, however, a sort of truce was established, and firing ceased. Just before I had rejoined my Regiment on the Chattahoochee, our pickets had been quite friendly with the pickets of the enemy. They had traded coffee for tobacco, and had offered to take letters and send them to Union prisoners in their hands. I should at this time have liked to send a letter to my brother. But now they would not go as far as that; nothing would induce them to meet us between the picket lines for trading; to all our advances they replied that their orders forbade them to do so.

On August 25 important changes were made in the disposition of our troops. Our Corps was withdrawn from before Atlanta and moved back to the Chattahoochee River. The rest of the army was moved around to the south of Atlanta, temporarily abandoning its communications; this was in order, by threatening his flank, to compel Hood to come out of his works and fight us in the open.

Throughout that day our heavy guns poured a constant stream of shot and shell into the city. As soon as darkness had settled down on the camps, we silently folded our tents and moved back. I had been on picket duty that night; it was still and clear, and the slightest sound could be heard at a great distance. As I passed along the picket line, from man to man, and gave them the word to follow instructions—which were for each man, as I passed him, to leave his post and go back silently to the rear—I could hear the Confederates changing their relief just a little in my front. In one case I heard the old sentinel tell the new one to "keep a sharp watch on those Yanks over there," for they were up to something and he believed they were going to attack.

At the railroad bridge over the Chattahoochee, where we took position, earthworks had already been built. We strengthened them and built new ones, so that by the night of the 26th we were in condition to fight the whole of Hood's army. Hood was, however, too busy south of Atlanta, where Sherman now was, to trouble us; and we had several days of complete quiet. It was a great relief, after our experiences in the trenches, to be able to walk around without hearing the bullets whistle about our ears. Not the least of our enjoyment was, to have a good river close at hand to bathe in.

During our stay here, General Slocum arrived and took command of the Corps. When he made his first tour around the camp, he was given a royal reception by his old command. They had all been anxious to have as their leader someone who had been identified with them in the Army of the Potomac. With that army they had won their laurels, and they wished still to be known as a part of it.

Slocum was a very different type of man from Hooker. The latter was brilliant and dashing, and in the excitement of battle his ardor and personal courage carried him where the fire was hottest. Slocum, on the contrary, reminded one of the descriptions of Marlborough. Cool and unimpassioned he directed a battle as he would a review. Without particularly avoiding danger, he would not rush recklessly into it. Hooker was an inveterate boaster. Slocum usually said nothing. I think most men would have considered Hooker the better leader, and Slocum the better man.

Late on the night of September 1, while I was on picket duty, I heard in the direction of Atlanta what I at first thought was artillery. The rumbling kept increasing in intensity until it seemed like the heaviest firing I had ever heard. Finally, a number of terrific explosions lit up the air. At six miles distance they seemed like bright flashes of lightning. I knew then that the enemy were blowing up their powder magazines. I supposed, however, that Sherman was fighting his way into Atlanta from the south.

At daylight a reconnoitering party was sent out toward the city. They found it evacuated, except for a small rear guard of cavalry which was soon driven out. The remainder of the Corps moved up in the afternoon, our Regiment reaching the city at about dark. Sherman's flanking movement had been completely successful. He had met Hood on the Macon Railroad, near Jonesboro, and had beaten him terribly. The Confederate commander had been obliged to evacuate Atlanta at once, blowing up eighty cars of ammunition which had been cut off by the capture of the railroad at Jonesboro. He had been compelled to destroy, also, the large rolling mill of the city, which was said to have been the only mill in the South where plating for gunboats could be manufactured.

We found more Union sentiment in Atlanta than anywhere else in the South. As our Brigade entered the city, at about nine o'clock at night, many of the women brought out buckets of water for us to drink. They were very bitter against Hood's army, which they said had robbed them of everything that could be carried off, with the excuse that the Yankees would steal it anyway. They were agreeably disappointed to find that the Yankees did not rob them of a thing.

Immense quantities of tobacco were abandoned by the Secessionist citizens who left town. This fact ruined the sutlers' trade in that article. On the day before Atlanta fell, tobacco sold in our camps at a dollar a plug, and fifteen cents for cigars. On the day after, plug tobacco passed about for five cents, and cigars were twenty-five cents a hundred. Our men found tobacco in every conceivable place. One lot of twenty boxes was dug out from under a big ash-heap. It was, however, the only plunder obtained, for the most stringent orders were issued against pillaging occupied houses.

The effects of the Union bombardment could everywhere be seen in the city. Almost every house had the marks on it of shot and shell. One man showed me a dozen shells that had struck in his garden. The families remaining in the city had all built in their yards bombproofs, to which they had fled for safety whenever the shelling was in progress.

On September 6 Sherman's army came back from Jonesboro, and went into camp in the vicinity of town. For a time we enjoyed the luxury of complete rest, after our four months of continuous campaigning. On September 23 our Regiment received from Wisconsin 200 fresh recruits, who had just been secured under the draft. Every one was a substitute, and a splendid lot of men they were physically, representing almost every nation in Europe—English, Irish, Scotch, Welsh, Germans, French, Norwegians, and I don't know how many others. Some of them could not speak a word of English. Over a dozen were full-blooded Chippewa Indians, who until they put on the uniforms of the United States Army, had never worn the clothing of civilized people. They were all excellent raw material, and in the course of time made good soldiers. I recall only two of the entire 200 who deserted.

About the first of October, Hood set out on his trip to the North, in the attempt to starve us out of Atlanta. On October 3 Sherman started after him with all of the army except our Corps, which was left to hold the town. Our camps were now changed around so as to defend the city on a shorter line. Our Brigade was moved from the south to the northwest side, and set to work to build new breastworks, or rather to rebuild the old ones of the Confederates.

The enemy succeeded in getting upon our railroad to the North, and for about twenty days we were completely cut off without news or provisions. However, they had left us the whole of the country southward to forage in; and this, together with the rice we had captured in the city, and the "beef dried on the hoof," as the men called the cattle that were driven in, kept us a long way from starving. Every week our forage trains would run out into the country to the south, and gather in from 500 to 700 wagon-loads of corn, besides living, while they were out, on the best that the land afforded. Moreover, we had our provisions all to ourselves; for on September 10 Sherman had ordered all the citizens of the town to leave either to the North or to the South.

On October 11 our Regiment went out for the first time on a foraging expedition. There were 2,500 men in the detachment, and a train of about 500 wagons. About fifteen miles south of Atlanta we found plenty of corn for the animals; and for the men, abundance of sweet potatoes and other dainties not laid down in the army menu. In two days we had our wagons laden with all that could be hauled away. About a fortnight later we went out again and brought in over 800 wagons of corn.

The forage which we thus gathered was the salvation of our animals and beef cattle. The mules had been on half rations of grain all summer, quite without hay, and the whole country in the vicinity of Atlanta had been grazed over until it was as bare as a city street. The beeves that had been driven down from Louisville, had for weeks nothing to eat save the leaves and sprouts on the bushes. It was a standing joke among the men that the commissary always killed for beef those animals that could not survive until the next day.

The March to the Sea

On October 29 came the first through trains from Chattanooga, after the movement of Hood to the North. On the same day came orders to reduce baggage and prepare for marching. Soon, rumors were spreading about the camp that we were to start on a fifty days' campaign, without communications. On November 4 we were ready to move. I wrote numerous letters of good-bye to friends at home, telling them that they would hear from me next at Charleston or Savannah. I hoped that it would be Charleston, for I wanted the people of South Carolina who started the war to feel its effects and to reap their share of the horrors.

On November 5 we started out and marched three miles from town. The next day, however, we returned in order to wait until the Army of the Tennessee might be paid off. This gave us a chance to vote in the Presidential election, which we had come very near missing. Our Regiment gave Lincoln 304 votes and McClellan 21. For another full week we remained in Atlanta, our Regiment being occupied the entire time in tearing up railroad tracks and destroying everything of value in the city. By the time we were ready to leave, Atlanta was worth little more to the Confederates than any other piece of ground of similar size. On November 15 we started out in earnest on the now famous "March to the Sea." Our last view of Atlanta, the prize for which we had so long struggled, was a column of dense smoke from its burning buildings; we had destroyed everything in town except the churches and private residences.

Our expedition numbered about 50,000 men, under the command of Sherman. Thomas's army remained behind to look after Hood. We took with us only about twenty days' rations, for the country through which we passed was expected to furnish the remainder of our needs. The army proceeded in two columns—the right wing under Howard making for Macon; the left under Slocum making for Augusta. Each corps, also, took a different route in order to be able to subsist more easily on the country.

Our Corps proceeded along the Augusta railroad, which we destroyed as we went along by burning the ties and twisting the heated rails. Parts of the country were poor and furnished little forage. Other portions, however, compensated by giving us an abundance of sweet potatoes and pork, with occasional lots of corn meal, flour, and sorghum, and, for the first arrivals on the plantation, chickens and turkeys. On our route we found plenty of good horses and mules, and all the forage that we could carry off. Occasionally, also the enterprising forager would capture some apple-jack or corn whiskey.

At Madison we turned and took the road to Milledgeville, the capital of Georgia. Geary's Division, however, followed up the railroad to the Oconee River, and destroyed the Oconee bridge. We entered Milledgeville on the 22nd without opposition, and camped in the state-house yard. During our stay, our Regiment and the One Hundred Seventh New York guarded the city. I took up my quarters with an acquaintance of one of my Wisconsin friends, and saw to it that his house and family were not molested. He had several hundred bales of cotton stored near town, which Sherman had consented to have bonded; but some zealous officer or officious "bummer," had set fire to it before it could be saved.

Upon our approach to Milledgeville, Governor Brown of Georgia, had released all of the convicts in the State Prison at that place. In celebration of their freedom, their first act was to destroy the old prison. Our first work was to destroy the Milledgeville arsenal, in which was stored a large quantity of Confederate arms and ammunition. We carried out and threw into the river, all of the ammunition in the magazine, and burned up all of the arms and equipment. Besides several thousand stands of good arms, there were a lot of old-fashioned rifles and shot-guns, and thousands of pikes and bowie knives that had been manufactured by the State for the militia, with which to repel Yankees. In the state-house were millions of dollars of Georgia State money, in bills of all denominations and to these the men helped themselves without limit. All of the cotton in the vicinity that could be burned without endangering good buildings, was destroyed, and that which was stored in the city was bonded not to be turned over to the Confederate Government, or used for its benefit. I was sent out with a detachment of men to search the stores for tobacco, and found enough to load several wagons, which kept the army supplied with that article until we reached Savannah.

From Milledgeville we marched eastward toward Sandersville, through a very poor country. At Buffalo Creek, a swampy stream about eight miles from Sandersville, we found that the seven bridges crossing it had been burned—the negroes told us that this had been done by the people of Sandersville. We were delayed about three hours in repairing the bridges, so did not arrive at Sandersville until the next morning. For the last two days we had been on slim rations, and Sandersville was well supplied. Of course there was a general rush for eatables, and the town was soon raided. The citizens hurried to Sherman to make complaint and get protection.

He turned on them and asked, "Which of you was it who set fire to those bridges yesterday?" They all denied having done it, but admitted that it had been done by citizens of the town. "Well," said he, "those that make war must take the consequences," which was all the consolation they got.

Later, we found the man who fired the bridges; he was promptly arrested and his property burned.

As we entered Sandersville we had a sharp skirmish with Wheeler's Confederate Cavalry, in which two of them were killed. Our Indians seemed to think it was not exactly right to leave the dead bodies with their scalps on. They soon fell into the civilized custom of making war, however, and did not afterward express any desire to take scalps.

From Sandersville we turned south until we reached the Georgia Central Railroad at Tennille Station. We burned the railway buildings there, and proceeded along the line, tearing it up as we went along.

On November 28 we passed near the home of the Honorable Herschel V. Johnson.[1] By prodding into the ground with their ramrods, some of our foragers found there a lot of more or less valuable papers and letters, which had for safe-keeping been buried in his cabbage patch. Some of the letters from his son, who was an officer on Hood's staff, afforded us much amusement. Our mess forager found here, also, a stock of flour that lasted until we reached Savannah.

Thus far, we had almost always found sufficient provisions along the line of march to feed the command fairly well. Now, however, we were obliged to send out strong parties of foragers for long distances on our flanks, to search the country in order to get enough to eat. Wherever we went we destroyed everything that might be of value to the enemy. On the 29th, near Bostwick, we burned up millions of feet of bridge timber, all got out and framed for bridges, that the Confederates expected to build when the Yankees were driven out. I noticed that some of the timbers were marked Strawberry Plains and Chattanooga Creek.

On December 3 our column crossed the Millen & Augusta Railroad near Millen, and destroyed as much of it as we could. We were now in a level, sandy country, thickly covered with pine timber, and plantations were few and scattered. On the 4th we heard cannonading in the distance, which was said by citizens to be at Charleston, South Carolina, seventy miles away. On the 7th we found our road for a distance obstructed with felled timber, which, however, so little delayed the march that those in the rear would not have known of it. On the 8th, after passing Springfield, the trains and pack-mules were left behind, with the Third Division as a guard, while the First and Second Divisions pushed on rapidly toward Savannah.

In Front of Savannah

We encountered the enemy in force for the first time fourteen miles from Savannah, in Monteith Swamp, where they had built an earthwork across the road and felled trees in front of it. The First Brigade of our Division was sent around to their left, and our Brigade to their right, while the Third Brigade moved forward on the center. Our plan was to hold their attention to the front, while we got around on their rear. They discovered us in time, however, to escape. Captain Kleven of Company H, who with his skirmishers, was in advance of our Brigade, made a rapid movement forward as soon as he saw the enemy falling back, and succeeded in capturing three prisoners. The First Brigade opened fire at about the same time, sending a few bullets over our way, and severely wounding in the foot, Captain Buck of Company B. The Third Brigade also came up in time to claim a share in the honor of capturing the three prisoners. Finally, to settle the dispute, the prisoners themselves were brought to Division headquarters, where they pointed out Captain Kleven as their captor.

At Monteith Station we captured the post-office and a considerable mail. The letters, which were mostly written by the soldiers whom we had tried to capture the day before, afforded the men an abundance of fun.

On the 10th we marched to within about four miles of Savannah, where we were stopped by the entrenched enemy. While we were getting into line, a detail of foragers, gathered along the banks of the Savannah River, spied a small steamer coming up the stream from the city. They hid themselves along the shore until the boat was directly opposite, when they opened a musketry fire and compelled the craft to surrender. It proved to be a Confederate dispatch boat on its way up the river to warn the fleet that Sherman and his army had arrived. The fleet did not receive the warning, and interesting developments followed. The men who had captured the prize did not know its value, and after stripping it of everything they wanted, set fire to it.

The country between our lines and those of the enemy was a big rice plantation, which overflowed at every high tide, and which could be kept under water by closing the flood-gates. The only means of access to the city were the narrow causeways built through this swamp. At the point where we were located, the Savannah River is divided by Argyle Island into two channels, the main or navigable one being near the Georgia shore. The island is about ten miles long, and at our end something like a mile wide. It was occupied by a large rice plantation, which naturally overflowed about two feet at high tide, but which had been ditched and diked so that the flow was regulated at the flood-gates. If we could control these, we could keep the island passable. The plantation buildings were situated on the east

side, near the channel, where a number of acres rose high enough above the general surface to be safe from overflow.

On the evening of the 11th our Regiment was ordered across to Argyle Island. There were on hand but two or three skiffs, and only a portion of the men could be brought over that night. In the morning the crossing was being continued, when suddenly the discovery was made that three steamers were coming around the bend of the river on their way to Savannah. Owing to the vigilance of our foragers on the previous day, they had received no warning of the presence of Sherman's army.

Captain Winegar of Battery M, First New York Artillery, had his rifled guns in position on a slight elevation along the shore, where he commanded the river for a stretch of nearly a mile. As soon as the steamers, which were a part of Commodore Tattnall's Mosquito Fleet, came into plain view, he opened on them. They probably had never before been under fire for their crews seemed confused. The first craft, which was a gunboat, commenced immediately backing and turning. The second, the armed tender "Resolute," started to do the same, but was run into by the third, and so badly crippled that she drifted ashore against Argyle Island. The other two vessels managed to escape up the river.

While the miniature naval battle was going on, our men who were on the island, under command of Captain Barager, had hastened to the scene. When the "Resolute" drifted ashore, they were on hand to prevent the officers and crew from making their escape in small boats, as they had started to do. There were twenty prisoners in all. We afterwards had a fine lot of fun listening to the officers as they accused one another of being the cause of the disaster. The "Resolute" was towed over to the Georgia shore, near the battery, but could not be repaired in time to be of any service in our future operations on the island.

The question of rations was at this time becoming vital. One day's allowance had been issued to us on the day after our arrival in front of Savannah. We were, therefore, on the lookout for anything that might serve to supplement our supplies. As soon as my Company had come across to the island, we took the shortest route to the plantation buildings on the east side. Not a thing was left; those who had come before us had already absorbed everything. But at the landing I found a good six-oared boat that would carry about ten men besides the rowers. Impressing a crew of negroes to row the boat, I started for a plantation on the other side of the river, about half a mile up, thinking that I would be the first man of Sherman's army to invade South Carolina. On landing, however, I was told by the blacks that two of our "bummers" had been there the day before, and in an altercation with the plantation hands had killed one of them. The funeral was just going on when we arrived. Subsequent events made me believe that Wheeler's Cavalry, and not our men were responsible for this tragedy.

I placed a sentinel out on the only road by which a mounted force could approach, and then began a search for eatables. We soon were rewarded by a good supply of sweet potatoes and sorghum. In the boat-house we found a fine lot of boats; as these were especially valuable for our purposes, we shoved them all out into the river to float down to our landing on the island. We had just loaded up our supplies, when my sentinel came running in with the report that a large force of cavalry were coming. We hastily pulled back to the island and waited for them; but they did not come to close quarters and soon retired.

Three days later I was sent out with Captain Barager's Company and my own to take possession of this plantation. We knew that the enemy now held it in some force, but we did not know how strong they were. I had secured boats enough on our first raid to be able to take over both of our companies at one time. We started in the morning, when it was as yet scarcely light, hoping to come upon the enemy unexpectedly. Their sentinels discovered us, however, and fired on us while crossing. We landed about a quarter of a mile from the plantation buildings and rapidly pushed forward. I sent Barager with his Company to the right, while I took the direct course to the rice mill, in which the enemy were sheltered.

The country was broken up into a mass of ditches, dykes, and canals. We found that our only road was along a narrow dyke, and that we should either have to return or charge them in single file. We did not retreat. In less time than it takes to tell this story, we had the mill. They gave us one volley and hit nobody. We did not fire a shot. They escaped with their guns and ammunition, but we captured all their provisions, including their breakfast cooking on the fire. For the first time in three days we had all that we wanted to eat. Colonel Hawley came over soon after, with three more companies, but toward night the Confederates appeared in such force that we again withdrew to the island.

The next morning the enemy brought down a section of artillery to the Smith Plantation, as it was called, and commenced shelling our island camp. I was sent with my Company to get as close as possible to them on our side of the river, and either silence them or drive them off. I got up within about a hundred and fifty yards of them and opened fire. They immediately turned their guns on us, and for a few minutes gave it to us hot. We had good shelter, however, and lost only one man—John Furlong, a veteran of

Company E. It took me about twenty minutes to drive off the battery, but their infantry held out all day.

On the 19th the whole Brigade crossed over to the Smith Plantation, with a section of artillery. Entrenchments were built at all commanding points, and preparation made to hold the position. On the 20th Colonel Hawley made a reconnoissance in force toward Union Causeway, the only Confederate outlet from Savannah, but found the enemy in such strength that he could not reach it. But from our position we could see the lines of their wagons leaving the city. On the morning of the 21st it was found that the enemy had evacuated Savannah, and our troops moved in and took possession.

We now received orders to recross the river to the Georgia side and march to Savannah. We had nothing but flatboats to cross in, and a strong wind was against us, so that we made slow progress while our Regiment covered the crossing. When all the rest had passed over, and we were about half embarked, the enemy swarmed down upon us by the thousand. They had us surrounded on three sides, with a river behind; and our chances for seeing Savannah were not brilliant. Nevertheless, we faced about and prepared to fight them. Our friends of the Second Massachusetts came, without orders, back to our assistance, and placed themselves where they could cover our flanks. We were sheltered behind a dyke, and the enemy could not get at us save by charging across an open rice field; this they did not have the nerve to do, so that when darkness settled down we got off safely to the island. I think there was not a man in our command, but thanked his lucky stars that it was not some of Lee's veterans that had us in that fix that night.

In Savannah

The next day, we crossed without interruption from the island to the Georgia shore, which we reached by four o'clock, and then marched toward Savannah. We went into camp on the bank of the river about two miles from the city, and this ended on our part the "March to the Sea."

Just twenty-five days had elapsed from the time our army left Atlanta until it signalled the fleet off the coast. During that time our wing had marched 300 miles, destroyed over 400 miles of railroad and an amount of cotton that can hardly be estimated, and most of the time had lived off the country. Of our immense train of 2,500 wagons not one had been captured on the route. We had moreover secured an almost entirely new stock of mules and horses. And to crown all, we had won Savannah with an immense amount of the spoils of war. It was everywhere the opinion that Sherman had struck the hardest blow at the Rebellion that it had yet received, and at the least cost. The troops were in high spirits over their continued successes. The feeling prevailed that they had but to start for a place, and it was theirs. The confidence in Sherman was unlimited. When we left Atlanta, on what was considered the most perilous movement of the war, I never heard a single expression of doubt as to our ultimate success. The Confederates whom we encountered considered him the ablest general that had commanded troops in the war, and feared him more than any other.

We remained at Savannah until January 17, 1865. Our camp was in a beautiful grove of live oaks and pine, festooned with Spanish moss, and the weather was delightful. The work was comparatively light, and the men were confidently looking forward to the end of the war. We built new fortifications around the city on nearly the same lines as the old Revolutionary works. New roads were constructed across Hutchinson Island and northward into South Carolina. We were also busy, in order that supplies might be brought in as fast as needed, in clearing out the Savannah River, which the enemy had closed with obstructions.

The citizens of Savannah seemed well pleased with their change of rulers. They uniformly treated us with courtesy, and displayed a sociability that we did not usually encounter in the South. In return, General Sherman showed them every possible consideration. I was never in a captured place where private property was respected and protected as it was here, or where citizens were allowed so many privileges. Employment was furnished to those who wanted it, and a large amount of provisions was placed at the disposal of the mayor of the city for distribution among the destitute.

A good story was told on the Episcopal rector of the town. He had been deputized by the rest of the clergy to wait on General Sherman, and get permission to preach. When he stated his business, Sherman at once replied, "Of course you can preach; that is just what I want you to do."

The preacher then stammered out an enquiry whether he would be compelled to pray for the President of the United States. "Pray for Jeff. Davis or the Devil, if you want to," replied Sherman; "I think you had better pray for them, for they need it more than Lincoln."

Marching Northward

On January 17 we crossed the Savannah River on our bridge of flatboats, and started on our new campaign to the North. We were at the outset met by such fearful weather that we were virtually brought to a standstill. Only a portion of our army had yet crossed to the South Carolina side, when a freshet of unprecedented height raised the river so suddenly that it swept away the bridge, overflowed Hutchinson Island, and carried off a lot of wagons and mules that were just about to start. The freshet came before there had been a drop of rain in our vicinity; but it began to rain immediately after, and it seemed as though it would never stop. The country everywhere became a perfect quagmire, and a dry spot was hard to find.

Slowly we proceeded up the east side of the Savannah River, the remainder of Sherman's army following on the right side. On the 29th, at Robertsville, we encountered a strong force of Wheeler's Cavalry, which delayed our column for a short time. Our Regiment was sent to the front to drive them off. The two right companies, under command of Captain Haskins, deployed as skirmishers, and soon swept the enemy away like chaff before the wind. On the 30th we opened communications with Sherman at Sister's Ferry, where he had brought the remainder of his army across into South Carolina.

We now left Savannah River, marching almost directly north. Profiting by our previous experiences, we early organized a foraging party of four men from each company. They had permission to mount themselves with captured animals as soon as possible. In a short time they not only had mounts, but sufficient pack animals to carry several days' provisions for the Regiment. The first time they came into camp they presented a motley appearance, riding horses and mules, and displaying every variety of saddle and harness known to man. But they were soon as well mounted as the cavalry, and had transportation and equipment for any service. As we marched northward, the enemy's cavalry became more and more active on our flanks, so that our foragers were compelled to unite for protection. Our detail and that from the Second Massachusetts, under Lieutenant Thompson, were united almost from the start.

The low ground and the constant rains made marching so difficult that we rarely covered more than twelve miles in a day. Much of the way we were obliged to corduroy the roads for the trains. For this purpose we used fence rails when they were to be had; when there were none, we cut timber and brush. Reaching the Charleston & Augusta Railroad at Graham Station on February 7, we spent the next four days in destroying the tracks toward Augusta.

While we were in camp at Graham Station, Colonel Hawley, who now commanded our Brigade, and General Slocum, our Corps commander, had an argument as to the best method of tearing up a railroad track. Hawley contended that it was best to line up the men along the track, and at the word of command have them pick it up and turn it over. Slocum protested that this could not be done. A bet was made of a bottle of Apollinaris water, or something else, and Hawley sent for his old Regiment to try the experiment. When the order came to fall in without arms, our men were cooking their supper. Captain Woodford of Hawley's staff went along the line, while we were forming, and explained that the Colonel had made a bet as to what the Regiment could do. We were soon lined up along the track, and the command was given to take hold and lift. In the hands of those brawny men, that railroad was a plaything. It went over so fast, that some of the staff officers who had gathered to watch the performance, had to move lively to escape the flying rails and ties.[2]

From Graham Station we marched northward through constant rain and mud, subsisting entirely on the country, without drawing rations except coffee or sugar, and generally we had plenty to eat; corn meal and bacon constituted our usual bill of fare. The army was in fine spirits. In thus picking up a living in such a country, where the only products of the soil seemed to be tar and rosin, and pitch pines the only visible vegetation, they felt confident of their ability to find a living anywhere.

Our Corps did not enter Columbia, but crossed the Saluda River about ten miles above. The Fifteenth and Seventeenth Corps of the Army of the Tennessee occupied the city, and destroyed everything in it. They released about sixty Union officers who were confined there; and between them and the soldiers and the whiskey that was found Columbia soon ceased to exist. Scarcely a private residence, even, was left. The only thing that would not burn was the new state-house, said to have been the finest in the Union, and this was mined and blown up. South Carolina was having a bitter taste of the horrors of war.

On February 21 we struck at Winnsboro the railroad running between Columbia and Charlotteville; and following this northward for a distance, destroyed it as we went along. Then turning toward the northeast, by way of Rocky Mount, Hanging Rock, and Chesterfield, we marched to Fayetteville, North Carolina.

During the entire march from Columbia to Fayetteville we had but three pleasant days; the rain was almost continuous. Our road, most of the way, was through swamps and creeks, where bridges had to be built and roads corduroyed. Frequently, from early morning until midnight, we worked in rain and mud to get our trains along for six or eight miles. The rough work soon wore out our clothing—many of the men were barefooted; many were wearing citizen's dress; the whole army looked more like Falstaff's ragged regiment than soldiers of the United States. But we met little opposition from the enemy. The spirit of four years before seemed to have been beaten out of them. We felt that the only Confederate troops that would still give us serious fighting, were those with Lee at Richmond.

Arriving at Fayetteville on March 12, we once more opened communication with the fleet, by way of Wilmington and Cape Fear River. On the 15th we set out on our way to Goldsboro, and the first night went early into camp, about ten miles from Fayetteville. At eight o'clock, however, we were sent out again into a dark and stormy night to go to the assistance of General Kilpatrick's Cavalry, which had met the enemy. For five miles we waded through mud and water to the place of danger, and bivouacked for the night in line, facing the enemy. In the morning we had some sharp skirmishing, but in the afternoon the enemy were driven from their position.

On the 19th General Carlin's Division of the Fourteenth Corps was attacked and thrown into confusion by General Joe Johnston's army near Bentonville. Our Brigade was rapidly pushed forward with a number of others, and formed in line of battle near the left of the Corps. The enemy made several attacks, the brunt of which fell upon the troops to the right, and then retreated. This battle, which the Union Army nicknamed the Battle of Acorn Run, in compliment to the badge of the Fourteenth Corps, was the last in which our Regiment was engaged during the war.

On the 22nd, we advanced once more, and found that the enemy was gone. Two days later we arrived at Goldsboro, and occupied the city without opposition. On the 27th, for the first time since we had left Savannah, rations were issued to the troops.

Peace

We began the last campaign of the war on April 10, entering Raleigh on the 13th without resistance. The next day we again began to organize our foraging parties, and to make preparations for a campaign back through Georgia. During the day, however, everything was changed. General Johnston, following Lee's surrender on April 9, had sent in asking for terms.

On April 20 I wrote home the following letter:

> Camp of the 3rd Wis. Vet. Infty.
>
> Raleigh, N. C., April 20, 1864.
>
> My Dear ——:
>
> The Angel of Peace has spread his wings over our country once more. The glad tidings were announced to the army last night by General Sherman in general orders. As

soon as the agreement which he had made with General Johnston and higher authorities could be ratified at Washington, peace would be restored from the Potomac to the Rio Grande. It was a glorious day for us who have seen the thing through from the beginning to the end. General Sherman also says that he expects "soon to have the pleasure of conducting this army to its homes," and I believe that within six weeks you will see me in Chicago "home from the wars."

I don't know just exactly what the terms of surrender are, but it is the opinion of high officers that no troops will be needed for garrison duty in the South. The rebels have been so completely whipped that they will never want to try another rebellion. I understand that Jeff. made no stipulation for his personal safety, but said he was willing to take his trial before the courts, and trust to the mercy of the American people. The only difficulty in the negotiations was on the question of the confiscation of landed property, and I have not learned how that was arranged. But I believe that we have been so completely victorious that we can afford to be merciful, and that a general amnesty will do more to cement the Union than the most rigorous punishment. The punishment that the South has already endured is like Cain's "greater than they can bear." The destruction of life in this war in the South has been terrible.

The news that Johnston had asked for terms on which to surrender his army was published on the 16th. On the morning of the 17th a gloom was thrown over the whole army by the announcement of the assassination of the President, which was reported to have occurred on the 11th. I never saw such a gloomy, sad time since I have been in the army as that. I don't think we knew how much we did think of him until then. Many expressed the opinion that if it had been Andy Johnson and Stanton, it would not have been much of a calamity. The next day we had New York papers of the 14th which made no mention of the murder, and we all thought we had been hoaxed. Then the explanation was made that the operator at Morehead City had made an error, and that the assassination had been on the 14th instead of the 11th, and now I hardly know what to believe about it. We shall probably get more news today.

We are about to move our camp, and now for the first time comfort instead of safety is considered in the selection. Just think of it! I can hardly realize it. No more skirmishing, no more digging trenches and building breastworks, no more whistling bullets, rattling grape-shot, or screaming shells, no more friends and comrades to be killed or wounded.

I don't know what has become of all my letters lately. The mail has come in here three times, and I have not had a letter. My last letters were dated in February, except one from * * * of March 7. I suppose they will all come in a heap one of these days. * * * The weather is very fine though almost too warm. We have occasional showers, and vegetation is growing fine. This part of North Carolina is very fine country and crops look well.

A great many of Lee's paroled army are coming in here, and they seem more pleased at being whipped or at getting home than we do at having gained a victory. Some of them say they cheered louder when they surrendered than Grant's army when they captured them.

Our camps were now overrun with citizens and paroled Confederate soldiers, who were hunting for horses that they had lost; some of them had come as far as sixty or seventy miles. We gave them all the spare horses that we had, for we knew that the Government would have to help them in some way to keep them from starvation. We also issued to them large quantities of rations, for there was nothing eatable left in all the track of Sherman's army. On the 29th, general orders were issued announcing the formal surrender of Johnston's army.

Homeward

On the next day began the march to Washington. We entered Richmond on May 11, and on the 15th camped near the old battle-field of Chancellorsville. On the 24th we marched into Washington, where the Union army passed in review before all the dignitaries of our Nation, the representatives of foreign lands, and the immense throngs of people who had gathered from far and near to see Sherman's veterans. For this review, we selected from our Regiment, eight companies of thirty-two men each—the best drilled soldiers that we had. It was my place to ride in the rear of the Regiment as it marched down Pennsylvania Avenue, and no command made a better show than ours. From the Capitol to the reviewing stand, the marching and wheeling were simply perfect.

We now went into camp near Bladensburg, where all of the men whose terms of service expired before October 1 were mustered out and sent home. On June 6, General Hawley issued his farewell order to the old Brigade. When it was broken up on the next day, the officers of the Second Massachusetts sent to the officers of our regiment the formal expression of the feeling with which they parted from us. We replied in a similar letter. Even now, after a lapse of twenty-six years, it stirs the blood to read these two messages.[3]

The Western veteran regiments still had work before them, and were not mustered out. They were organized as a provisional Brigade under Hawley's command, and ordered to Louisville, Kentucky. Our Regiment left the east on June 11, travelling by way of the Baltimore & Ohio Railroad to Parkersburg, and then down the Ohio River to Louisville. Here the Regiment was filled up with men from other Wisconsin commands, that were mustered out of service, until we had about 1,500 on our muster rolls. It was rumored, and in fact intended, that we should go to Mexico to drive out the French. The programme was entirely changed, however, when news came of the voluntary withdrawal of the French soldiers, and orders were issued to muster out our Regiment.

A considerable number of our old veterans did not want to go home. A company was made up of those who wished to enter the services of the Juarez government in Mexico—at least they wished to go, if I would go in command. I was not quite ready, however, to become a soldier of fortune. When our duty to the Federal Government had been accomplished, I was as anxious as any to be mustered out of the army of war, and return to the army of peace.

INDEX

FOOTNOTES

[1] H. V. Johnson was born in Burke County, Georgia, in 1812. He served his State as Federal Senator from 1848 to 1849, and as Governor from 1853 to 1857. In 1860 he was nominated for the Vice-Presidency on the ticket of Stephen A. Douglas. He opposed to the last the secession of Georgia, but ultimately cast his lot with his State, and was elected to the Confederate Senate. After the war he was active in securing the restoration of Georgia to her political rights in the Union. In 1866 he was again chosen to the Federal Senate, but was unable to serve under the reconstruction acts of Congress. He died in Jefferson County, Georgia, in 1880.

[2] A detailed description of the manner of destroying railroad track during Sherman's Campaign is given by Gen. H. W. Slocum, "Sherman's March from Savannah to Bentonville," in *Century Magazine* Old Series, xxxiv, p. 930.

[3] This correspondence was as follows:

Second Massachusetts Infantry,

Camp Slocum, Washington, D. C,

June 4, 1865.

We, the undersigned, officers of the Second Massachusetts Infantry, wish to express to the officers of the Third Wisconsin Infantry our heartfelt regret that the fortunes of the service are about to separate our respective organizations.

From the campaign of 1862, in the Shenandoah Valley to the present glorious close of this bloody war, we have fought and marched side by side with you in almost every rebellious state. To have been brigaded together for so long a time is in itself remarkable; no less so is it that between our two regiments there should always have existed such strong feelings of friendship and mutual regard, untinged by the slightest shadow of jealousy.

As we recall now, some of the hard positions we have been in, we cannot help remembering how often our anxiety was lessened by the knowledge that the old Third Wisconsin was close at hand to support us. We know that you have had the same thoughts about us. Nothing in this whole war will be pleasanter for us to look back upon than this feeling of mutual respect and reliance. It not only elevated the tone of both our regiments, but we honestly believe, it went a great way toward making our brigade and division what they are now acknowledged to be—among the very best organizations of the army.

We assure you that in our own State, wherever the Second Massachusetts is known, its brother regiment is also famous. Whenever any of us have been at home, among the first inquiries would be, "How is the Third Wisconsin?" It has been with pride that we have answered, "It is the same staunch old regiment that fought at Antietam and Chancellorsville."

These are not compliments but expressions of plain, honest feelings. We have been knit together by deeds not words; deeds, which, as time goes on, we shall look back upon with continually increasing pride.

Together we have shared dangers and hardships, victories and defeats; and it is hard now for us to part; but in the natural order of things, the war being over, you go towards your homes in the west, we stay near ours in the east. Let us not, however, though separated by thousands of miles, forget these old associations. Let us rather cherish them with the fondest recollections: let it be a story to hand down to our children and children's children, how the Second Massachusetts and Third Wisconsin fought shoulder to shoulder through the great rebellion, and achieved together glory and renown. We ask you to accept this testimonial as a slight evidence of our affection and esteem. We bid you farewell, and God bless you, one and all,

C. F. Morse, Lieutenant Colonel, Com.; James Francis, Major; C. E. Munn, Surgeon; John A. Fox, Adjutant; E. A. Hawes, Quartermaster; Captains—Daniel Oakey, F. W. Crowninshield, E. A. Phalen, George A. Thayer, Theodore K. Parker, Dennis Mehan, Henry N. Comey, William E. Perkins; First Lieutenants—George J. Thompson, Jesse Richardson, Moses P. Richardson, William T. McAlpine, Jed C. Thompson, William D. Toombs.

Third Wisconsin V. V. Infantry,

Camp Slocum, near Washington, D. C.

June 7, 1865.

To the officers of the Second Massachusetts Veteran Volunteer Infantry:

The undersigned, officers of the Third Wisconsin Veteran Volunteer Infantry, tender their heartfelt thanks for your friendly communication of the 4th inst. It was with mingled feelings of pride and pleasure, not, however, unmixed with pain, that we perused it—pride at being thus associated with a regiment, which by patient endurance, good discipline, and unflinching bravery, has won for itself so honorable a name as the Second Massachusetts; pleasure at the thought that, even amid the stirring scenes of active war, the finer attributes of humanity are not forgotten, and that friendship, one of the noblest sentiments of the soul, still asserts her claims; pain at the recollection of the many gallant and brave, whose names have been associated with yours in the great struggle now happily terminated, but who have given their lives for a country they loved so well.

That "every rose has its thorn" was never more apparent to us than now. While in the toil and suffering of our active campaigns, we have looked forward with unmixed joy to the time when the angel of peace should once more spread her wings over the land, and we should return home to enjoy the sweets of social and civil life, but now that the hour is at hand when we must say farewell to those with whom we have been associated in the service of our common country, when we must join the parting hand with you, our companions and brothers in arms, our joy is mingled with sadness and our smiles with tears.

We accept your communication, not only as a manifestation of personal regard, but also as a fraternal greeting from the east to the west, which rising superior to local jealousies and factional strife, and remembering only the mingled dust of our dead on many battlefields, and the common country for which they sacrificed their all, proclaims us, in heart and in country, one and inseparable.

In parting, we assure you that, highly as we prize this expression of sentiment toward us, and sacredly as we will preserve it as the highest honor yet received, it is not needed to secure remembrance. The ineffaceable pictures of the past deeply engraven in our hearts, and lit up by the eternal flame of friendship will ever keep the Second Massachusetts Veteran Volunteer Infantry prominent among our pleasing memories in the future.

Wishing you all success and happiness and Heaven's best blessing, we bid you farewell. We are, brothers, yours fraternally,

George W. Stevenson, Lieutenant-Colonel; Warham Parks, Major; J. G. Conley, Surgeon; T. J. Kopff, Assistant Surgeon; A. C. Taylor, Adjutant; J. T. Marvin, Quartermaster; I. E. Springer, Chaplain. Captains—Ralph Van Brunt, Julian W. Hinckley, N. Daniels, E. Giddings, A. D. Haskins, C. R. Barager, J. Woodford, John M. Schweers, John E. Kleven. First Lieutenants—Stephen Lieurance, Oliver A. Hegg, J. D. Goodrich, John Agnew, John B. Du Bois, Abner Hubbell, J. D. Babcock, W. W. Freeman, George H. Cutter. Second Lieutenants—E. V. Moran, Lewis Colby, Edwin F. Proctor, Elon G. Biers, David Clark, A. S. Hill.